Also Available From the American Academy of Pediatrics

Caring for Your Baby and Young Child: Birth to Age 5 *(English and Spanish)*

Heading Home With Your Newborn: From Birth to Reality

Mommy Calls: Dr. Tanya Answers Parents' Top 101 Questions About Babies and Toddlers

The Wonder Years: Helping Your Baby and Young Child Successfully Negotiate the Major Developmental Milestones

Your Baby's First Year *(English and Spanish)*

New Mother's Guide to Breastfeeding *(English and Spanish)*

Food Fights: Winning the Nutritional Challenges of Parenthood Armed With Insight, Humor, and a Bottle of Ketchup

A Parent's Guide to Childhood Obesity: A Road Map to Health

Guide to Your Child's Nutrition

ADHD: A Complete and Authoritative Guide

Waking Up Dry: A Guide to Help Children Overcome Bedwetting

A Parent's Guide to Building Resilience in Children and Teens: Giving Your Child Roots and Wings

Sports Success R_x! Your Child's Prescription for the Best Experience

Less Stress, More Success: A New Approach to Guiding Your Teen Through College Admissions and Beyond

Mental Health, Naturally: The Family Guide to Holistic Care for a Healthy Mind and Body

Caring for Your School-Age Child: Ages 5 to 12

Caring for Your Teenager

Guide to Your Child's Allergies and Asthma

Guide to Toilet Training *(English and Spanish)*

For more information, visit www.aap.c

D0288637

RAISING TWINS

From Pregnancy to Preschool

Shelly Vaziri Flais, MD, FAAP

American Academy of Pediatrics
DEDICATED TO THE HEALTH OF ALL CHILDREN™

American Academy of Pediatrics Department of Marketing and Publications

Director, Department of Marketing and Publications
Maureen DeRosa, MPA

Director, Division of Product Development
Mark Grimes

Manager, Consumer Publishing
Carolyn Kolbaba

Director, Division of Publishing and Production Services
Sandi King, MS

Editorial Specialist
Jason Crase

Print Production Specialist
Shannan Martin

Manager, Graphic Design and Production
Peg Mulcahy

Director, Division of Marketing
Jill Ferguson

Manager, Consumer Product Marketing
Kathleen Juhl

Director, Division of Sales
Robert Herling

Cover design by Cathi Stevenson, BookCoverExpress.com
Book design by Peg Mulcahy
Illustrations by Tony LeTourneau

Library of Congress Control Number: 2008940544
ISBN: 978-1-58110-344-1

CB0056
9-127   1 2 3 4 5 6 7 8 9 10

🐦 What People Are Saying

Dr Flais, from her own experiences, will teach you how to simplify, synchronize, and customize parenting your twins. Her "Twin Tips!" will help all families. As she says, "Your best ally during your twins' early years is their need for *sleep*." Amen.

    Marc Weissbluth, MD, FAAP

    Author of *Healthy Sleep Habits, Happy Twins*

Raising Twins is a must for anyone raising multiples! It's filled with huge amounts of advice from both an experienced pediatrician and a fellow mom of multiples! I especially recommend her "Twin Tips!" for fast reference. This is a great book for anyone expecting multiples and those immersed in their early years. I highly recommend it.

    Denise M. Anderson

    President, Illinois Organization of Mothers of Twins Clubs, Inc.

Tandem feeding, duo sleeping, twinproofing, and double discipline are only a few of the many tips on raising twins covered in this handy must-have parenting guide. Pediatrician and mom of twins, Dr Flais shares a double dose of practical information that I recommend all parents of multiples read before delivery and keep close at hand during the first few years.

    Tanya Remer Altmann, MD, FAAP

    Author of *Mommy Calls: Dr. Tanya Answers Parents' Top 101 Questions About Babies and Toddlers* and editor in chief of *The Wonder Years*

Double your pleasure but save time, stress, and money! *Raising Twins* helps parents of multiples hit the ground running and build their skills, efficiency, and confidence. A mom of twins and 2 singletons herself, Dr Flais also shares tips on celebrating your twins' "twinness"—as well as their individuality. This practical resource is a necessity for anyone caring for twins!

Jennifer Shu, MD, FAAP

Coauthor of the award-winning books *Heading Home With Your Newborn: From Birth to Reality* and *Food Fights: Winning the Nutritional Challenges of Parenthood Armed With Insight, Humor, and a Bottle of Ketchup;* medical expert on CNNhealth. com; and editor of *Baby & Child Health: The Essential Guide From Birth to 11 Years*

Want to be a stress-free parent of twins or multiples? Read this book!

Gale Gand

Cookbook author, host of the long-running Food Network show *Sweet Dreams,* executive pastry chef/owner of Tru restaurant, and mother of twins

Who better to hold your hand and help prepare you for the multiple joys (and challenges) of parenting twins than a pediatrician-mother of twins? By combining a medically sound foundation with a reality-based approach, *Raising Twins* is sure to provide new and expectant parents of twins a double dose of valuable advice and insight.

Laura A. Jana, MD, FAAP

Pediatrician; coauthor of the award-winning books *Heading Home With Your Newborn: From Birth to Reality* and *Food Fights: Winning the Nutritional Challenges of Parenthood Armed With Insight, Humor, and a Bottle of Ketchup;* and an identical twin!

To all families with multiples, and to my beloved husband and children.

ಎ✲ Table of Contents

Chapter 6: The Toddler Years (1- and 2-Year-Olds).. 107

Chapter 7: The Preschool Years (3- and 4-Year-Olds)... 143

Chapter 8: The Early Years End—As Your Twins Grow 169

ꙮ Acknowledgments

I have many people to thank for playing a special role in my life and in the development of this book. The opportunity to write this book has been a complete joy and honor, as it combines the passion I have as a pediatrician to help other parents raise their children happily and healthfully with the practical knowledge I have gained while raising twins in addition to single-born siblings close in age.

I thank my amazing husband Mike, Michael J. Flais, MD, for being a constant source of love and support. I thank you for being the most wonderful husband, partner, and father to our children. Your humor and steadfast calm help us through any challenge in life.

I thank my 4 children for teaching me most of what I know about parenting—I am so lucky to be a mom to such awesome kids. Matthew, with a lightning-quick mind, you can explain Cassini's mission to Saturn's moon Titan, then tell a joke about lawnmowers running on "grass-oline." Andrew, you take pride in taking care of your family members with your sweet smiles and hugs. Ryan, you are as cool as a cucumber, even-keeled with a hilarious sense of humor. Nancy, you are vivacious and wise beyond your years.

I thank my mother and father, Nancy and Ira J. Vaziri, MD, for decades of illustrating good parenting by example. My brothers and I learned that we can accomplish even our loftiest goals with dedication and hard work, whether our goals are to become an eye surgeon, create amazing visual effects for landmark movies, or help other parents navigate the world of multiples.

I thank our extended Vaziri and Flais families for their love and support.

I thank Sarah Lacey Pilarowski, MD, FAAP, assistant clinical professor at the University of Colorado School of Medicine Department of Pediatrics and community pediatrician at Cherry Creek Pediatrics, for her invaluable peer review of book content, as well as a rewarding long-term friendship.

I thank Kristina Ferro Keating, MD, FAAP, of Lake Forest Pediatric Associates in Lake Forest, IL, for her invaluable peer review of book content and years of friendship.

A big thanks to the wonderful people at the American Academy of Pediatrics for their guidance and expertise—Mark Grimes, director, Division of Product Development; Carolyn Kolbaba, manager, consumer publishing; Kathy Juhl, manager, consumer product marketing; and the entire production team.

A hearty thanks to the numerous wonderful families with multiples who helpfully shared their notes with me during the process of writing this book—the Orrico family, the deGuzman family, the Dooyema family, the Winkler family, the LaMonte family, the Peters family, the DeRome family, the Graf family, the Sayles family, the Hynek family, and the Long family.

And I thank you, the reader—congratulations on joining the ranks of families with multiples! Our multiples community is amazingly supportive of each other through all the challenges and triumphs of parenting twins, triplets, and more. In *Star Wars: Episode VI: Return of the Jedi,* Yoda asked of Luke Skywalker, a well-known twin, "Pass on what you have learned." Spread the love and pass on the lessons *you* have learned to other families with multiples.

❧ CHAPTER 1
Introduction

One beautiful August day, the skies were blue and the sun was shining. "Can we take our training wheels off our bikes, please?" Mom and Dad had heard this request countless times before—and on this clear day, my identical twin boys' summerlong pleas were finally answered. My husband and I, managing a busy family with 4 young kids, had been hesitant to remove our safety net of the training wheels. Were the boys ready to make this adjustment?

Ryan's bike was first. Being fascinated by tools and gears, he watched intently as Dad removed the unwanted support system. Eager to practice, he hopped on his streamlined bike and quickly learned that starting and stopping required some new adjustments. Once he gained momentum, however, there was no stopping him! With Ryan happily practicing his new skills, it was Andrew's turn. Andrew had waited patiently and cheered Ryan's success—twins learn, with experience, how to take turns nicely! Within moments, each boy was off and cycling, starting to get a good feel for a new way of riding the bikes.

As I watched each of my boys race past me on the sidewalk, I felt a strange sensation. I felt as if it was just a week earlier that we learned we were pregnant with twins. How is it that we went from seeing 2 heartbeats on an ultrasound to watching these 2 amazing, unique kids whiz by on bicycles, all in the blink of an eye?

❧ Your New Life With Twins

If you are expecting or are already parenting twins, congratulations! If you are nervous about the challenges of raising twins, remain calm and take a deep breath—you can do it! You may be unsure of your abilities to parent multiples, but you will quickly adapt to your new family dynamic. You'll spend your twins' first year or so synchronizing the babies' schedules to make life easier. As your twins grow, you will nurture each of your twins as an individual. And in the blink of an eye, your twins will be riding their bikes in figure-eight patterns around you!

More and More Twins!

More and more multiples (twins, triplets, and more) are born every year. The National Vital Statistics System reports that twin deliveries rose 42% between 1990 and 2004. Whether your twins are conceived naturally or via fertility treatments, the news you are carrying multiples can be quite a shock!

As a child learns to ride a bike without training wheels, she has some initial adjustments to make as she figures out a new way of cycling. Similarly, as parents welcome twins into their family, they adjust and learn a new way of managing family life. You will soon get a feel for how to handle your new life, twins included, and be cruising along, free of your training wheels!

How will you handle more than one baby? You can care for twins or more by remembering the basics of good parenting. A good parent provides love, safety, and security. Babies only need a few things—something to eat (breast milk or formula), something to pee and poop into (diaper), a safe place to sleep (crib), and a safe way to ride in the car (car safety seat). If you streamline your newborns' needs, you will be able to provide what is important to your twin babies.

When you have twins, triplets, or more, the most important mantra to remember is to *keep the babies on the same schedule.* It is the best way to happily survive your twins' first year of life! When one wakes up to eat, it doesn't matter how cute the other guy looks sleeping—you have to wake them both up for the feeding. If the babies' feeds are not coordinated, you could easily spend the entire 24 hours of any given day feeding them, one after the other. If you feed 2 babies on 2 different schedules, you will not be able to sleep a little bit, spend any time with an older child in the family, or recognize that vaguely familiar-looking person over there who reminds you of your spouse.

ஃ The News Flash of a Lifetime

Your reaction to the news that you have more than one baby on the way is most likely a mix of strong emotions. I will admit that the first month after discovering that I was pregnant with twins, I felt like a deer in the headlights. How could I be having twins? How on earth could we handle 2 newborns at once?

You and your spouse may have very different reactions. While I was nervous, my husband was thrilled and breezily optimistic. He told me, "Relax, it will be great! Everything will work out just fine." I appreciated his joy and confidence, but I felt frustrated that he wasn't showing fear of the unknown, while I felt unsure of my ability to handle the situation. I wondered just how steep our learning curve would be to find our groove.

If I only had a time machine back then, I could have relaxed a bit. Here we are, a few years later, and not only have we survived, but we have very much enjoyed our twins' early years. I had been so nervous when pregnant that I imagined it would be more difficult than it actually is to raise twins. In reality, the day-to-day routine of taking care of 2 little babies at the same time is very doable! Once your family starts using some strategies to streamline your twins' care, you'll be able to breathe more easily and enjoy the whole process.

The challenges of raising twins are what make the parenting successes even sweeter. It is fascinating to watch as each twin's unique personality evolves and develops over time. The highs and lows of the parenting experience are amplified for parents of multiples. You'll have moments of intense exhaustion, but also moments of unsurpassed joy.

Have faith in yourself and your parenting abilities. The human spirit has an amazing ability to rise to a challenge. You can successfully parent twins, one day at a time. Any challenge in life must be tackled one step at a time, and twins are no exception. One particularly tough day may feel like it lasts an eternity, but soon a time will come when you look back and wonder how the early weeks and months flew by so quickly!

➤ How the Parenting Experience Changes Over the Early Years

The job of parenting multiples will require different skills from you at different stages. The earliest weeks and months with twins will require stamina and an ability to streamline your daily tasks to survive with some semblance of sanity remaining. As time wears on, you can ease out of survival mode and shift gears into a different skill set. You will become a master of understanding human emotions and interactions as you navigate all the different personalities that live under your roof. You'll have as good of a grasp of interpersonal relations as any diplomat!

Pregnancy

During your twin or triplet pregnancy, you'll want to channel your nervous energy into preparing your nest for your babies. Twins and all multiples tend to deliver earlier than single-born babies, so you'll want to prepare in case this happens. Of course, another reason you should prepare early is because your belly will get quite large and uncomfortable as you approach your due date. You can start attending your local twin club meetings to meet other parents of multiples and start collecting helpful tips. Pregnancy is also the time to enlist family and friends for help in the early weeks and months of your twins' lives.

Early Infancy

During the twins' newborn period, your family will adjust quickly to a brand-new routine. The daily schedule will be filled with feedings, burpings, diaper changes, and catnaps, cycling through the days and nights. You and your newborn twins will begin a relationship with each other that will strengthen with your love and consistent responses to their basic needs. You may discover during this period that while your babies were born at the same time, they may have 2 very different temperaments and personalities. If there are older siblings in your family, you'll want to continue to shower love and positive attention on them as well, to help them feel as much a part of the process as possible.

Later Infancy

During the twins' later infancy months, you'll be coaxing everyone into a more predictable schedule, and kids and parents alike will know what to expect at certain times. Your twins are becoming little people and you are starting to see what makes each of your twins tick.

The Toddler Years

When your twins are toddlers, life is overall much easier to handle, but you've got some major milestones to negotiate, such as toilet training and transitioning to big-kid beds. Strategies that work for single-born children need to be tweaked a bit when you're toilet training 2 kids at the same age in the same home. All toddlers are starting to realize that they are independent people, separate from their parents and their twin. As a parent, you'll be helping your toddler twins make more decisions for themselves within an acceptable framework of behavior.

The Preschool Years

The preschool years with twins are such a great payoff for your years of effort! Your home evolves into your twins' imagination factory. The twins sleep all night (for the most part!); they use the toilet to pee and poop (for the most part!); and you're now able to really enjoy them even more and nurture each of them as unique individuals. As your twins grow, you will see one of the many benefits of having twins is that their twinship taught them about patience and sharing; the twin experience provides built-in life lessons. Many experts believe that twins may be more socially savvy than their single-born peers because of the relationships they've grown with since infancy.

Enjoying the Parenting Experience

Parenting twins can be quite hectic, and in the early days and weeks, parenting twins can consume your full days *and* nights. You don't want to merely *survive* raising twins; you want to enjoy the experience, retain your sanity, and maintain a good relationship with your spouse and other children. Each day is only 24 hours long. Of all the tasks and events in a given day, there are the mundane things that we must do to keep the home running, and then there are the fun bonding experiences we'd like to enjoy more. Instead of folding laundry all day, it would be nice to have a moment to cuddle with your twins and read them another good book.

As a parent of twins, you'll need to strategize, plan, and organize to streamline the everyday, necessary tasks as much as you can. That way you can have more time and energy to simply *be* with your twins and *enjoy* them. Another part of the equation of happy parenting is finding time to nurture yourself, spend with friends, exercise, and nurture your relationship with your spouse. A happy parent is a better parent. It is not selfish to seek out personal or couple time—it is healthy and will have positive effects on everyone in the family.

Not all of us can afford to hire babysitters or outside help on a regular basis, and not all of us have available family nearby who are able to help make our personal or couple time a routine experience. But with some simple strategizing and creative planning, you can carve out such time.

Implementing and maintaining a routine household schedule. will go a long way toward protecting special time for your twins, your other children, yourself, and your spouse. Your best ally during your twins' early years is their need for *sleep*. Young children need plenty of sleep. If the family works together to maintain a routine bedtime for the kids once they have grown past the newborn stage, you will have a couple of hours every night for couple time, or at least the ability to think a complete sentence in your head without interruption!

⤳ Families With Twins—One Size Does Not Fit All

My firsthand experiences taught me a lot as a parent and as a pediatrician. Our oldest son was only 18 months when our identical twin boys were born! My husband and I had to quickly figure out how to care for 3 kids, all younger than 2 years. Efficiency became our middle name as we coaxed ourselves and our 3 young sons to operate on a daily schedule so that we could all survive. We were both practicing physicians and had no outside child care assistance—he handled our sons solo on the days that I worked in my pediatric practice, and I handled the boys solo on his working days. Our fourth child, a daughter, born a month before our oldest son turned 4 years old, rounds out our family.

I continued to practice clinical pediatrics part time through my twins' toddler years, and then made the decision to stay home temporarily while my 4 children were young. I can appreciate twin parenting from both perspectives—working outside the home, pumping breast milk and all, and being at home as the children's primary caregiver. My professional knowledge and real-life experience with 4 young kids has helped me to efficiently, healthfully, and lovingly parent, and I appreciate the opportunity to share some of my insights with you and your family.

That being said, there will be friends, family, and health care professionals giving you advice and encouragement as you embark on *your* journey with twins. Listen to what everyone has to say and give some ideas a try, but ultimately, only you can figure out what will work for your family and your situation. Not all families with twins are the same. A family with 2 older kids and twins will need to operate much differently than a family of solely twin children or a family with twins and one younger sibling. Accept the support and camaraderie of others, but *you* as the parent will find what works for your individual family. Listen to others' advice, but have confidence in your own parenting judgment and abilities. You will not only *survive* your twins' early years—you will *enjoy* them!

CHAPTER 2

Preparing for Your Twins' Arrival

*L*et's get an ultrasound just to be safe." I hadn't expected to be strolling my first son, still just a baby, toward the ultrasound suite during the first routine prenatal visit for my second pregnancy.

My husband and I always hoped to raise a big family. We were eager to get pregnant again soon after our first child was born. Happily, our home pregnancy test soon turned positive, and at the 6-week mark I brought baby Matthew along to visit the obstetrician for what I thought would be a straightforward second pregnancy checkup.

I mentioned to my obstetrician that I had had some minimal bleeding, but was otherwise well. Apparently the bleeding was enough to warrant an ultrasound.

Matthew and I entered the small ultrasound room. The tiny room was toasty warm from the large ultrasound machine and other running equipment. As we began the study, Matthew began to fuss in his stroller, so I hoisted him up onto the examination table with me and held him tight as I tried to lie flat on my back. Matthew was finally content when he saw how fun it was to swat at the crinkly examination table paper with both hands. I securely held onto Matthew so he wouldn't fall, which is no small feat during an uncomfortable vaginal ultrasound.

The ultrasound technician seemed to be taking quite a while with the study. I busied myself with Matthew. "Hmm…well, that's what I thought. OK, take a look at this," she said as she turned the monitor so I could see it.

When you're looking at a fuzzy, moving, black-and-white image, it is challenging to interpret what you're seeing. But what I saw on that screen was unmistakable—2 tiny spots flickering repeatedly, each to its own rhythm. Two hearts! The world stopped, as I was sure I just stepped into someone else's life. Utter shock and disbelief. I hadn't planned on twins. I plan everything—this wasn't part of my plan!

Through my dizzy blur of emotions, clutching onto a wriggling, oblivious Matthew, I kept focusing on those 2 blips on the screen. They were so beautiful, so innocent, sending their rhythmic beats across the ultrasound waves like communicating stars in the Milky Way. I was mesmerized and terrified at the same time, all the while having what felt like an out-of-body experience.

☙ The Emotional Roller Coaster

Congratulations! You are about to enter the world of twins. This world is an amazing and remarkable place in which you will share many beautiful moments in your twins' lives. It is also an experience that can be chaotic and challenging, but have faith! Just as generations of parents have survived and succeeded, you will as well. Unexpected joys will be yours as you watch your twins grow and develop relationships with each other and everyone in your family. Becoming a parent changes your life forever, but becoming a parent to twins is truly a gift.

You will never forget the moment you learn that you are pregnant with twins. Whether you conceived the babies naturally or with fertility treatments, the reality that you are already the mother to 2 growing, living beings is amazing. You may be very emotional about the news. Pregnancy, with all of its associated hormones, is already an emotional time! The fact that you'll have 2 bundles of joy can increase the emotions even more so. You may feel elated and joyous one moment, anxious and panicked the next. It doesn't matter if your pregnancy was a surprise or has been planned for years—your emotional roller coaster is completely normal.

Preserve your emotional well-being by discussing your feelings with your partner, your family, and your friends—anyone who is a good listener. Your excitement can transform into fear in mere moments, and discussion with loved ones is the best way to sort out your feelings and begin devising coping strategies. Make good use of your support network as a sounding board for what you are experiencing.

> ## Twin Tip!
> Talk about your emotions during your twin pregnancy. Seek out good listeners to support you during this exciting time.

Your support network includes family and old friends. You'll also be meeting new families at your multiples prenatal classes and at your local Mothers of Twins (MOT) club meetings. Of course, your family and older friends know your history, and you may be able to share your deepest fears with your family. You may also find that your new friends who are pregnant with or already have twins relate to your situation better. It is very comforting to talk with someone who is living a similar experience to yours! There are advantages to different kinds of support.

Ideally, the people you include in your support network should be positive and upbeat. Many well-meaning people may put their feet in their mouths when they learn that you are expecting twins. These people are as surprised and shocked as you, and when they learn the news, they may have poorly thought-out remarks or questions. In most cases, these people mean well and are simply blurting out their comments without realizing that they might be insensitive. Inconsiderate remarks may feel hurtful to you, especially in your state of emotional overdrive. Try not to let these comments get under your skin. People may ask if twins run in your family, or if you used fertility treatments—you can simply respond vaguely, "We are very surprised and happy." The nature of your children's conception isn't anyone else's business.

Another option is to respond with humor. One mother I know had a standard response whenever anyone asked her, "What are you going to *do?!*" She would reply, "I'll just sell one of them on eBay!" The absurdity of this response alerts the questioner that she has asked an unhelpful and silly question. If you prefer to give a less sarcastic response, just let this person know that you wouldn't have conceived twins if you couldn't handle raising twins. Everything happens for a reason! Most importantly, after your witty or concise response, leave it at that. You don't need to get into details with the offender, and it will not help your emotional state to have this kind of conversation. If certain people in your life cannot be upbeat and supportive about your twin pregnancy, you may need to maintain some emotional distance from those people for your sanity. Now is the time to take care of your body, your emotional status, and your babies.

You may feel scared at times, but remind yourself that you are up to the task. Human nature has an amazing ability to adapt. Even though you may not have expected twins, have confidence. It is important, however, to envision your life with twins realistically. Don't expect to become the perfect twin mother. There are no perfect mothers, even of single-born children! You are going to do the best you can. Your main job will be to provide love and a nurturing environment for your twins.

Twin Tip!

Have confidence in your ability to raise twins. The characteristics of good parenting are universal, whether you have 1 or 2 babies. If you can provide love, food, and safety to your babies, you can successfully parent twins.

Your local MOT club meetings are a great source of support. Even if you cannot attend on a regular basis, it can be quite informative to be surrounded by a room full of women who are expecting or already have twins. This is important because people who haven't lived it just cannot relate to the crazy experiences you're about to have! During my twin pregnancy, I was very worried about how young my first son was, and the fact that he would only be 18 months old when the twins would be born. I met a woman right away at a MOT meeting who was due to have her twins around her first daughter's first birthday! I had been thinking I'd be the only mom in the country with 3 kids younger than 2 years, and suddenly here was a room full of people who could relate. Meeting these other moms diminished my feelings of isolation. You may feel alone and scared, but if you reach out, you will find other twin families who have not only had a similar situation, but also *survived* it and are richer people for having had the experience.

You should also take time to let go of your plans for a straightforward single-baby pregnancy. We have all daydreamed for years about the perfect, typical singleton baby and about the way that baby would fit into our lives and families. It is quite an adjustment to any preconceived hopes to learn that you will have 2 little babies entering

> # Twin Tip!
> Seek out advice from other families with twins. You are
> not alone!

into your life and family at the same time. Allow yourself time to
let go of the old fantasy. Twins may not be what you expected or
planned, but twins have a way of providing you with happiness
and love that you never thought possible. You are in for the treat
of a lifetime.

When you feel overwhelmed or even sad that you are expecting
multiples, the feelings of guilt are not far behind. "All my friends
have it so easy, having just one baby at a time. It would be so much
easier to give birth to just *one* baby than have twins. But I shouldn't
feel this way, shame on me. How can I feel sad when I am so lucky
to be having twins?" You are human and entitled to not always be
happy. Allow yourself to feel the full range of emotions as need be,
and let go of the guilt. If you feel disappointed at times, acknowledge
your feelings and then move forward. Use this time to talk with your
partner. Also, get cracking on your to-do lists. A good way to relieve
some stress is by using your nesting instincts to prepare for your
twins' arrival.

Taking Care of Your Body and the Pregnancy

The fact that you are carrying more than one baby does place you
in a special category in the eyes of obstetricians. Many would call
a twin pregnancy a *high-risk* pregnancy, but don't be scared by this
categorization. High risk does not automatically translate into your
pregnancy having problems. Rather, high risk can be translated as,
"We will need to follow this pregnancy more closely." Also in the
high-risk category are mothers with diabetes, those with a history
of preterm labor with prior pregnancies, or those who have other
major health issues themselves. The majority of twin pregnancies
progress smoothly, and the odds of a healthy pregnancy increase if
you take better care of yourself.

The most important step to care for your pregnancy is proper nutrition. Ideally, pregnant mothers should take a prenatal vitamin with folic acid starting from 3 months prior to conception. Folic acid has definitively been proven to reduce the chances of neural tube defects such as spina bifida. If you haven't started taking the vitamin daily yet, don't fret about the missed time—but do start now. Take the vitamin with food to reduce nausea, and applaud yourself for taking yet another step to keep your babies as healthy as possible. Moms of twins don't need 2 prenatal vitamins a day—one is enough.

Eating the proper foods and the right amount of calories is critical in a twin pregnancy. Whereas single-born pregnancies require 300 extra calories a day, most experts agree that twin pregnancies need around 1,000 extra calories a day. Frequent and healthy snacks can help you reach your caloric goals each day. Morning sickness—or in most women's cases, all-day sickness—can be eased by eating small snacks frequently. Keeping a little something in your stomach at all times can help take the edge off of the nausea. Low-fat yogurt, fruit, smoothies, crackers, and protein shakes are all good snack options.

In addition to the extra calories, it is important to sip on water throughout the day. Keeping well hydrated may drive you crazy in later months when it seems like you're running to the bathroom every 5 minutes; however, your babies' extra blood flow and removal of wastes depends on it! It may help to drink more water earlier in the day and then stop after 8:00 pm so that you can sleep longer stretches at night between bathroom breaks.

Twin Tip!

Remind yourself to drink plenty of water even during a busy day at work. Every morning, pre-fill your daily water needs in individual water bottles or a bigger container. Take sips of water every hour. At the end of the day, empty bottles will tell you that you drank what you needed.

Proper nutrition and hydration is important for your twin pregnancy, as is listening to your body. Any new pregnancy symptoms you notice *must* be brought to your obstetrician's attention; seemingly minor things could be a sign of something more serious.

Because twins have an increased chance of being born early, any symptoms or concerns *must* be addressed for the safety of your babies. Bleeding or vaginal discharge, contractions that are becoming more frequent, pressure in the pelvis or lower back, or even diarrhea can all be signs of preterm labor. And while early bleeding in the first trimester could be the normal phenomenon of the twins implanting in the uterine wall, you should call your obstetrician if you experience bleeding at any point.

Twin pregnancies can also increase the chances of preeclampsia, a condition in which the mother has increased blood pressure, protein in the urine (detectable by urinalysis), and more swelling than is normal in pregnancy. If you notice rapid weight gain or headaches, alert your obstetrician so you may be examined as soon as possible. Depending on the severity of the situation, treatment may range from bed rest, to hospital-administered medications, to immediate delivery of the babies (the only "cure" for preeclampsia).

An optimistic yet careful attitude during your pregnancy will help your mental state and hence help your babies thrive during pregnancy as long as possible. Take things one day at a time and one week at a time. Eat well and pay attention to what your body and your twins are telling you. Every extra day that your babies spend inside the womb will help them once delivery day arrives. The bigger your belly gets, the bigger your smile should be, since you're creating 2 miracles!

Twin Tip!

Have you heard of TTTS? It stands for twin-to-twin transfusion syndrome. It is a rare occurrence for identical twins (10%–20% of monochorionic twin pregnancies, meaning identical twins who share one placenta). The 2 babies' blood can mix in a connection between placental vessels, resulting in one baby receiving too much blood, while the other baby receives too little. Prenatal ultrasounds can study the placenta, blood flow, and growth and development of the identical twins.

🐾 Pregnancy Preparations

The more you do now to prepare for your twins will help immensely once your twins arrive. If you are on a form of bed rest because of pregnancy complications, you will need to delegate preparation tasks or use the Internet as much as possible. Consider obtaining necessary items, such as cribs, a bit earlier in the pregnancy than you would for a traditional singleton pregnancy because it is entirely possible that the babies will decide to show up early.

Attend MOT club meetings if you can. Even 1 or 2 useful tidbits of information may really help you out. That one tip you learn could potentially save you hours of time and effort down the line. It was at a MOT club meeting that I learned about a twin-feeding pillow, a large device making it easy to nurse or bottle-feed both babies simultaneously. I had never heard of twin-feeding pillows, even though I was a pediatrician! This single tip made our family's lives amazingly easier those first few months. I cannot imagine surviving the early weeks without my trusty twin-feeding pillow. At twin club meetings you'll hear these tidbits of information as well as meet other women who are in the same boat. You will learn how other families with twins have survived and prospered. Twin clubs also host clothing and equipment swaps as well as sales of gently used items from other members. Real bargains can be found at these sales.

You must shop carefully when preparing your nest for twins. The baby product industry would have you believe that you need 20 pairs of baby booties, a dust ruffle for the crib, a baby wipe warmer, and a diaper pail for every room in the house. Advertisers even go as far as to publish "handy" checklists with many unnecessary or irrelevant items. Feel free to use these lists as reminders or guides, but don't feel obligated to buy all the items on them.

Twin Tip!

A twin-feeding pillow will simplify simultaneous nursing or bottle-feeding of your twins; refer to the Twins' Preparation Checklist later in this chapter to find one.

First-time parents especially need to be aware of the baby product marketing phenomenon. Because it is your first baby or babies, you want to prepare as best you can—that is what being a good parent involves, right? Baby product companies take advantage of new parents' feelings of anticipation, anxiety, and inexperience by subtly hinting that if you are to be a good parent, you'll definitely purchase the crib mobile with the alphabet on it for just $49.99. Expensive things are not what make you a good parent! A good parent provides love, safety, and security. All the other bells and whistles are just extras; keep this in mind as you prepare your budget.

> ## *Twin Tip!*
> Is your head spinning over too many must-have baby items? Many baby products are not necessary. As long as you have food, diapers, cribs, and car safety seats, you're set. Anything else is a bonus.

Parents of twins need to make budgeting a priority—you'll note how expensive it is requiring 2 of everything at the same time. You will have to buy or launder twice as many diapers, and you'll need twice the bottle supplies if you are pumping or not nursing. You will probably need to streamline other areas that are negotiable. It is important to note, however, that over the long haul, twins are not much more expensive than 2 babies born separately; it's just that you'll need certain things at the same time. Now is the time to start asking for help. Send a call out or mass e-mail to your extended family and friends, inform them of your soon-to-arrive twins, and ask for baby items to borrow.

Borrowing baby items is wonderful because a lot of baby gear has a limited life span and is only usable for a few months. Bouncy seats, carriers, and baby swings are quickly outgrown. For example, a soft-pack front carrier can start to be used around 8 pounds (check the specific manufacturer's instructions), up to around 20 pounds, which can be by 9 months. Don't be overly particular about hand-me-downs. I remember during my first pregnancy, I wanted to buy everything new and fresh for my son. Months later, after numerous

Twin Tip!

When preparing your nest for twins, stay on a budget by borrowing extra baby equipment.

spit-ups, I realized, hey, it really isn't a big deal to borrow a baby swing and save some cash.

When it comes to toys, consider Internet-based companies that rent age-appropriate toys to families. Once a batch of toys is outgrown, it is mailed back and a new, age-appropriate set of toys is mailed out. A toy-rental service is a creative way to save on costs as well as reduce clutter and minimize waste. Investigate different ways to streamline your budget.

Other must-have baby items are probably not necessary at all. You'll have to decide for yourself whether certain items are worth buying to have a cute nursery or if you'd rather save the money and hassle. A good example is a crib bumper—it may surprise you to learn that a bumper is not necessary. Babies usually do not roll over for the first 3 or 4 months, so you don't need to worry about them hitting their heads on the rails. Then soon after 6 months, many kids start to grab the rails, trying to climb up on the bumper, and at that time you'll need to remove the bumper for safety. Is it worth having a bumper for a month or two? Do you really need to worry about laundering the bumper and reattaching it every week or so—more frequently if it was spit up on? I say no thanks; life with twins is hectic enough. Now is the time to streamline your life and prioritize.

Make sure you carefully examine and clean borrowed equipment to ensure that it is safe. Verify that there are no loose or broken parts. When you borrow items, you also need to make sure they are not on any safety recall listings. Check out the US Consumer Product Safety Commission Web site at www.cpsc.gov to make sure your borrowed items have not been recalled. This is especially important for cribs because your twins will probably spend most of their time there.

When acquiring the necessary equipment for your twins, use the Internet as much as possible. If you are pregnant and on house arrest (bed rest), or even after the delivery of your newborn twins, it is a lifesaver to have an Internet lifeline available to help. Housebound

> ## *Twin Tip!*
> Make sure that borrowed or secondhand baby gear has not been recalled by checking the US Consumer Product Safety Commission Web site.

by your twin pregnancy or infant twins, it is gratifying to be able to point and click on your computer and have the things you need delivered to you. A little research will help you figure out who offers free or low-cost shipping. Many parents even find ordering drugstore necessities or groceries online for delivery to be helpful for the first few months after the twins arrive. If you are the lucky recipient of a twin baby shower, many Web sites can help you set up a shower gift registry online, saving you repeated trips to the store.

?❧ Twins' Preparation Checklist

I cannot stress this enough—babies need your love and hugs more than stuff or cute outfits. That being said, here is a list of items babies will need, along with items you may not necessarily need but will save your sanity. This list is not all-inclusive, but includes important points for the parents of twin babies to remember in the early months. Items useful later in your twins' lives will be discussed in subsequent chapters.

- Crib or cribs. Your twins will sleep most safely and comfortably in 2 separate cribs. Either buy 2 new cribs, or just 1 if an older sibling has outgrown his or her crib that meets current safety standards. If a trusted friend or family member has an extra crib you can use, great, but do your homework and make sure the crib is not on a safety recall list. Any crib's slats should be no wider than 2⅜ inches.
- Car safety seats. You definitely need 2 of these. A car safety seat is the one item (or should I say 2 items?) you should not borrow or take a hand-me-down. If a car safety seat has been involved in even a minor accident, it must be replaced. New car safety seats have a LATCH (Lower Anchors and Tethers for Children) system that makes proper installation much easier if you have a newer

car that is LATCH-ready. You can install your car safety seats by LATCH or by seat belts; make sure you read your specific car's owner's manual carefully for instructions, as well as the instructions that come with the car safety seats. Because twins are small at birth, you'll need an *infant* car safety seat, preferably with head and neck support. Don't worry about convertible car safety seats until later, as your newborns will probably not be the designated minimum weight at birth.

- Breast milk or formula. Ideally this will be breast milk in the beginning weeks of your babies' lives, but you may want or need to use infant formula to supplement breastfeeding or feed exclusively. We will discuss breast milk and formula feeding issues at length in later chapters.

- Bottles, nipple rings, and silicone nipples. You'll find that a dishwasher will make cleaning these much easier. The sanitizing settings on most modern dishwashers will effectively sterilize your equipment for you. Small plastic dishwashing baskets can hold the nipples and nipple rings in place during a dishwashing cycle. Also make sure that you have newborn slow-flow nipples on hand (there are medium- and fast-flow options for when your twins have grown). Newborns typically feed on breast milk 8 to 12 times in 24 hours (on formula, a little less frequently), so you should estimate your needs and know that you may need as many as 16 nipples in 24 hours. You could always have less, but then you'll need to wash the used nipples several times throughout the day. If you'll be using a breast pump, make sure your bottle supplies are compatible with the pump.

- Breast pump. A pump is infinitely useful if you plan on nursing your twins. If you find that you need to boost your milk supply, pumping will help stimulate your breasts to produce more milk, and you can store your precious, nutritious milk for a later feeding. A high-quality electric double breast pump will be worth the investment when it saves you time and energy collecting breast milk. Many moms choose renting a breast pump rather than buying one up front—rentals allow parents a little more flexibility in the budget. Breastfeeding twins will be discussed further in subsequent chapters.

- Diapers. Disposable diapers are quite convenient but expensive. Log onto major diaper manufacturers' Web sites to obtain coupons for parents of twins. You may need to wait until you have birth certificates because some companies want proof that you actually have twins. Many families use cloth diapers and launder them themselves or use a cloth diaper service. The cost and availability of these services vary from region to region, so you will need to do some investigation. Cloth diapers can be more environmentally friendly than filling up landfills with all the disposables, but cloth does require energy and water usage for all the washings.
- Twin-feeding pillow. I recommend getting a twin-feeding pillow before you are 6 months pregnant so that you are ready in case the twins deliver early. The twin-feeding pillow is a wonderful yet simple invention that makes simultaneous feeding much easier. It is helpful for breastfeeding and bottle-feeding your twins. I used mine from birth to about 7 or 8 months of age. Enter "twin feeding pillow" into your Internet search engine to find some great examples. Feeding the twins at the same time saves time and helps keep the twins on the same daily schedule.
- Changing table. Once you have changed a few diapers while slouching over the bed or the floor, you'll realize the health and comfort of your back may depend on a changing table. Even if you have a safety strap on the changing pad, *never* step away from the table, even for a moment. Even a newborn can wiggle her way off the table if you are not there holding a hand on her. Our family mounted a changing pad on a dresser upstairs so we could have one changing area upstairs and one downstairs. A second changing table is not a necessity, but it sure made life easier those first few months!
- Clothing. Do you prefer to let laundry pile up and deal with it once a week? Or do you prefer to launder more manageable piles more frequently? Your answer to these laundry questions will help you decide how much clothing to obtain for your twins. For clothes to wear at home, no one cares if your twins stay in pajamas all day. Do plan for spit-ups and diaper overflows; you may need 2 or 3 outfits a day per twin depending on the day's activities! Babies grow fast, so don't buy too many newborn-sized

clothes—these may be outgrown quickly. Important clothing and
layette items include

— "All-in-one" shirts that snap closed at the crotch, as well as
separate tops and bottoms

— Socks (shoes are not needed until the babies are walking)

— Footed pajama sets

— "Sack"-like pajamas with an open bottom hem to simplify
overnight diaper changes

— Receiving blankets for swaddling

— Baby washcloths and hooded towels for bath time

- Infant washtub for bathing.
- Twin stroller. There is a range of prices and styles for twin strollers. Tandem front-back strollers are more convenient for younger
babies because you can often snap the infant car safety seats right
into the stroller. Front-back twin strollers are also narrower and
hence easier to get through doorways for your pediatrician visits
(which are more frequent in the first months). Side-by-side strollers are nicer for older babies and toddlers because the twins can
interact more in this style. Side-by-side strollers are wider than
the tandem front-back strollers and do not fit through standard
doorways, but they usually fit in doorways wide enough for a
wheelchair. The more expensive options can be quite lightweight,
so if you live in a city and use your stroller every day you may
want to make this investment. Be sure to check the stroller's baby
weight minimum and maximum rules to be sure your babies will
be safe in the stroller.
- Waterproof mattress pads to protect crib mattresses. In addition,
smaller waterproof pads placed on top of the crib sheet makes
cleaning after spit-ups or other spills much easier. You simply take
away the soiled pad and replace with a fresh pad, saving the time
of remaking the entire crib with new sheets.
- Front-pack carrier or sling. These carriers have a limited life span
but can make your life easier trying to get things done around the
house. A second carrier means your partner can carry the other
twin and no one gets jealous! Baby slings are another great option.
- Play yard(s). These are useful for keeping your babies safe in
different areas of your home when you need to answer the phone
or run to the bathroom. Some models come with a changing table

attachment so that you can have a diaper changing station in your main family area; extra diapers, wipes, and burp cloths can be stored in the lower compartment.

- Digital camera. With twins, you'll take countless pictures, but only a small proportion of all shots taken may be photo-print worthy. Especially with twins, the more babies in the picture, the more likely someone will be moving and have a blurry face. You will save money in the long run if you can select which pictures should be printed. Be sure to get a large memory card for the camera so you needn't worry about the number of pictures you're taking in a session.

Twin Tip!

Take plenty of pictures of each of your twins *alone,* as well as together—they will thank you later for treating them as individuals. How can you remember who is who in the pictures? Color-coding their clothes will help you identify them years later, if you aren't able to label the photos in a timely fashion. Boys and girls lend themselves to different color codes pretty easily. Girl-girl twins can use purple for one and pink for the other. Boy-boy twins can wear blue for one and red for the other. Or, one twin can wear primarily solid colors while the other wears prints or stripes.

- Diaper pail with deodorizer system. Diaper pails trap odors with varying degrees of success. Breast milk stools really don't have much of a foul odor, so if you are nursing, a diaper pail may not be necessary. In my experience, when solid foods are started around 4 to 6 months, the diapers really start to emit a stronger odor that even the best pail can't cover up. Our family found it easiest to store dirty diapers in an ordinary lined trash can kept inside the garage, away from our noses.
- Rocking chair or glider. Once your twins are strong enough, they can sit on your lap with support while the 3 of you read a book together. This is especially nice as part of your nighttime routine

to help signal to your twins that it will soon be time to sleep. In the early months you will probably need your partner's help in picking the twins up when you have finished reading, but you'll find yourself becoming more self-sufficient with such tasks as time progresses.

- Bulletin board or comparable organizational system. It is important to keep track of infant twins' feedings and soiled diapers, and record keeping can quickly become overwhelming. Have a system for recording your babies' feeds, wet diapers, and poopy diapers in a central location of your home. If you weren't already an organized person, don't worry—parents of multiples become quite organized very quickly to keep up with everybody's needs!

Twin Tip!

The bullet-pointed Twins' Preparation Checklist
- Two cribs
- Two car safety seats
- Breast milk or formula
- Bottles, nipple rings, and silicone nipples
- Breast pump
- Diapers
- Twin-feeding pillow
- Changing table
- Clothing
- Infant washtub for bathing
- Twin stroller
- Waterproof mattress pads
- Front-pack carrier or sling
- Play yard(s)
- Digital camera
- Diaper pail with deodorizer system
- Rocking chair or glider
- Bulletin board or comparable organizational system

> ## *Twin Tip!*
>
> When preparing older siblings for the birth of twins, *books* are a terrific resource. Age-appropriate books are an excellent way to help any child of any age through a multitude of transitions.

⤳ Preparing Older Siblings

The arrival of a new baby creates a whole new family environment, requiring adjustment on behalf of all family members. With the arrival of twin babies, the new family dynamic changes even more dramatically. Older siblings' lives will invariably change with the arrival of 2 newborns that rely on the parents to take care of all their needs. The proper way to prepare your older child for the twin birth depends on her age and developmental level.

If your child will be younger than 2 years when the twins are born, you will be dealing with a little less of sibling rivalry issues. Toddlers younger than 2 are much more adaptable and seem to take the birth of a new baby more in stride. The greatest challenge is for children aged 2 to 3 years. Older than 3 years, the child has a better understanding of what is going on; however, he still craves lots of love and attention from his parents, as any child does.

In the first trimester before the pregnancy begins to show, you may want to hold off on explanations to children younger than 3 years. A good time to periodically talk about the arrival of new babies is after the pregnancy has passed 12 weeks and you are starting to show. Toddlers especially enjoy picture books of babies, and age-appropriate baby doll sets are a fun way to pretend play before the babies' arrival. Keep in mind that it will be difficult for your child to imagine life with the twins until it actually happens.

Once the twins arrive and come home, they will mainly require feeding, changing, and snuggling; all this can be accomplished while you engage your older child in conversation and play. The twins' language development will benefit from observing mom and the older siblings chat. Let the twins relax in their bouncy chairs and watch while you and their big sister work on a craft project together, for example.

It is important to try to avoid major lifestyle changes for older siblings around the time that the twins are born. Becoming a big brother or sister is enough of a lifestyle change for a young child already! Now is not the time to transition your older child to a big-kid bed, for example. If a room trade must be made for space issues, make the trade earlier in the pregnancy so your child does not feel he has been replaced by the twins. If your child has been potty trained, you might expect some accidents. Regressive behaviors during the adjustment period are normal and common as a child adjusts to life with 2 newborns in the family. You will have a lot on your plate caring for 2 new babies, and you might find yourself frustrated if your older child is acting out as a call for attention. Be as understanding of your older child as you can be, as challenging as that may be given all your new responsibilities.

If sibling rivalry issues take hold, make sure to make time for one-on-one attention with your older child. He can go shopping with just mom, have bath time with just dad, or have other "together" fun activities that you enjoyed before the twins' birth. Daily special time together, apart from the twins, will go a long way to reassure your older child that he'll always be loved. Even if you don't have babysitting for the twins to take your older child on an outing, you can use the babies' nap times for special one-on-one time with your older child. Newborns sleep most of the 24 hours in a day, so this will allow more time to spend with your other child than you may think. Of course the big challenge, which will be discussed in subsequent chapters, is to help the twins sleep *at the same time,* so that everyone can live a healthier life.

Nearing the Delivery

As you advance through your twin pregnancy and prepare for your twins' big arrival, your belly will expand as you've never thought possible. Your big belly is illustrative of your growing and thriving twins. As challenging as carrying twins can be, savor each day of your pregnancy. Each day in the womb is so critical for your twins' development. Applaud yourself for eating well and keeping the twins healthy. Start packing your hospital bag early, get lots of rest, and put your feet up at every opportunity.

CHAPTER 3

The Early Days and Weeks

When your delivery day finally arrives, you will likely feel a mixture of relief and newfound trepidation. The months of wondering what the deliveries would be like, wondering *when* the deliveries would happen, and perhaps some time on bed rest are now at an end. One chapter is closing while a new chapter begins. Yikes! Your twins are here!

In the Hospital

The babies may have been born full term, or they may have delivered prematurely. In either case, rely on your hospital staff for guidance and advice. Neonatal intensive care unit (NICU) nurses and newborn nursery staff members bring a wealth of experience and knowledge to the table. Avail yourself of the hospital staff's advice at every opportunity. The nurses have seen it all. There is no such thing as a silly question, especially if you are a first-time parent.

Allow the overnight staff to care for your twins so that you can get some nighttime sleep, recover from the births, and prepare for your homecoming. You shouldn't feel that you have to do it all while you are in the hospital. You are still recovering from the births yourself, and if you cannot recover properly, you will not be able to care for anyone else. Think of the emergency procedures on an airplane— first you must put your own oxygen mask on, and then you can help others with their oxygen masks. You cannot effectively care for your babies if you are not operational yourself. There will be plenty of time for you to do it all when you are back home with your babies! Soon you will be home, wishing you had someone to ask if your babies' poop looks normal or if you're burping them the right way.

Twin Tip!

Ask plenty of questions when you are in the hospital after the birth of your twins. With all the excitement, labor, and sleep deprivation, you may forget your important questions, so keep a pen and notepad by your bedside to jot down your thoughts for later.

While you are in the hospital, the newborn nursery nurses can show you their techniques to swaddle a newborn, which is one of the most important lessons for a first-time parent. Even seasoned parents can use a refresher course in good swaddling techniques. Lactation consultants can help you with the breastfeeding process. They can help your babies figure out how to latch on correctly, show you different ways to tandem-feed your twins, and show you how to pump and store your precious milk. The NICU nurses will help you learn how to administer medications if your babies will need them.

All too soon, you will find yourself loading up your babies in their car safety seats, discharge papers in your hand, with the all clear to take your babies home on their maiden voyage outside the womb.

₴ Coming Home

Bringing your newborn twins home from the hospital can be a relief. It is good to return to your familiar, comfortable home, bed, and nonhospital food. But then the realization hits—we have 2 little babies to take care of! Where are the helpful nurses and hospital staff with their extra hands? Take a deep breath and take things one day at a time. The babies will get stronger and bigger every day, and your family will learn a new way of living that includes your new twins. Think of life with your twins as a great sailing adventure on the high seas. Your homecoming is when you start to learn to tie knots and hoist the sails. You're just hitting the waters now, and soon you'll achieve a cruising speed and be sailing on an amazing journey!

A word about your homecoming—if your twins have older siblings, now is a great time to celebrate them and to view the twins' arrival from their viewpoint as well. I recommend discussing the new babies in the most positive terms as possible with your other child. "Here are your new little sisters. How lucky they are to have you as a big sister!" Lavish as much attention as you can on your older child. The babies have no idea if you're talking to them anyway, but your older child does! You'd be amazed at the great conversations you can have with an older child while you are burping your twins. Extend the philosophy to others—when well-meaning relatives and friends visit to coo over your adorable newborns, remind them

> ## *Twin Tip!*
>
> Your twins' births means that your older child is now a big brother or big sister. Some families like to highlight older kids' new title by giving them a big-sibling gift from the new twins to commemorate their new family status.

ahead of time to please say hello to your older child *first* and to include him in the conversation as much as possible!

🐚 Keeping Your Twins on the Same Schedule—Starting Now

How will you survive your twins' first weeks of life? Well, the good news is that newborns sleep a *lot*. Eating and sleeping are the 2 main concerns of any newborn baby. The key to *your* survival is to make sure that your twins start sleeping at the same time! On average, newborns need 16 or 17 hours of sleep in a 24-hour day. The inconvenient aspect of this sleep is that it is evenly divided into daytime and nighttime sleep, with frequent interruptions for feeding. All newborns need to eat at least every 3 hours because their stomachs are so small, yet their caloric needs so great. Breastfed babies may need to eat every 1 to 2 hours in occasional cluster feeding. Frequent nursing sessions help boost your milk supply and accommodate for your child's growth spurts.

So how do you coordinate the chaos of 2 babies needing to eat and sleep in such frequent spurts? Here is the golden rule for feeding twins: *when one wakes up to eat, both must wake up to eat.* Your heart may break to wake up a sleeping baby, especially when she looks so cute and precious lying there sleeping, but remember that you will not have enough hours in a day to feed one after the other is fed, day in and day out. Once the babies are awake to eat, feed them at the same time, with burp breaks throughout and a good burping session at the end. If you have a helping hand to feed one twin while you feed the other, great. But if you are breastfeeding, or ever plan on being alone with your twins, you'll need to teach yourself how to feed both babies simultaneously. You might as well start learning now!

> ## *Twin Tip!*
> The golden rule for feeding infant twins: when one wakes up to eat, both must wake up to eat.

The best way to feed both twins simultaneously is with a large twin-feeding pillow, which works for nursing and bottle-feeding (figures 3-1 and 3-2). It is a large U-shaped pillow with a firm foam core that fits around your waist and an opening at the back. Most versions have a safety belt to latch in place so that the pillow remains snug to your body. Each twin gets his or her own side and feeds in the football hold position. You will likely need help positioning the babies on the pillow in the early days but you will learn how to position them by yourself with time. You will soon be very capable, handling both babies safely simultaneously. If you've had a cesarean delivery, you may need to wait a week or so before starting to use a twin-feeding pillow because the pillow's front edge

Figure 3-1. Double football hold position for breastfeeding.

Figure 3-2. Double football hold position for bottle-feeding.

crosses your healing abdomen. In the postoperative period, use bed pillows propped on both sides to nurse your twins in a double football hold position. An alternative breastfeeding position has one baby in the traditional cradle hold and one baby in the football hold (Figure 3-3).

Positioning standard bed pillows or throw pillows for each feeding is a nuisance in the long run to get the right fit each time for frequent newborn feedings. It is critical that you position yourself and the twins properly for feedings, whether breastfeeding or bottle-feeding, to prevent backaches from poor posture.

Figure 3-3. Alternative breastfeeding position with one baby in traditional cradle hold and one baby in football hold.

Hunching over for 20 minutes at a time, 8 to 12 times a day, can really take its toll on your body!

Every baby is different, and each set of twins is different. I will present a suggested twin newborn schedule here. Feel free to tailor this schedule to your own twins' needs. When your twins wake up to eat, look at the clock and make a mental note of the time. Newborns often can only tolerate being awake for an hour or an hour and a half at a stretch, 2 hours tops. The fact that they can only be awake roughly 90 minutes at a time can help you adjust your twins to live on the same schedule. How is the time awake spent? Feeding and burping will take quite some time (especially as mom and dad work on positioning the babies correctly). After feeding and burping, the twins should get some time upright to help them digest their milk; this is a nice time to interact and play with them. Bouncy chairs are helpful to keep one baby upright, safely buckled in, while you cuddle or burp the other twin.

Twin Tip!

Whether breastfeeding or bottle-feeding your twins, take the time to make sure you are properly positioned to prevent aches and pains down the line.

Usually the post-feeding time is an ideal pooping time for babies due to the *gastrocolic reflex*—food in the stomach stimulates the bowels to move. If you wait a bit after feeding to change diapers, you may save a diaper by anticipating the stool in advance and waiting for it. After all the feeding, the burping, and the diaper changing, take another look at the clock. I can assure you it is probably almost time for the twins to go back to sleep. They may not appear particularly fussy, but remember that crying is a late indicator of fatigue. Don't wait for a newborn to cry to put her down to sleep—at that point, she will be overly agitated and stimulated by the crying. You will learn to identify your babies' more subtle clues that they are ready to nap. Swaddle your twins in receiving blankets to mimic the womb environment. At this point, they are fed, burped, and have a clean diaper, so they have nothing left on their agenda but to go back to sleep for a couple of hours.

Twin Tip!

Coordinate your newborn twins' schedules. Eat, burp, play, change diaper, sleep…eat, burp, play, change diaper, sleep…and repeat! One of your twins may always be the baby to wake up from his nap hungry for milk. You are not scarring his twin for life by always waking him up to eat with his brother! You are helping him by maintaining his parents' sanity. If you coordinate your twins' schedules, over time each twin's internal clock will align with the other twin's clock, and they will naturally get hungry at similar times.

Then, after a good nap (meaning more than one hour), when one of the twins wakes up, watch the clock. If the other hasn't awoken within 10 minutes, wake him up as well and proceed with the plan again. You can see the emerging pattern. Repeating these cycles of both twins waking up, eating, burping, playing, changing, and going back to sleep is how you can handle 2 newborns at once. Manipulate this suggested schedule to fit your own needs, but make sure that you stick to your version of the schedule! Consistency is the key.

> ## *Twin Tip!*
>
> When feeding newborn twins during the night, be as boring as possible! Leave the lights low and do not talk or sing to your babies. They will start to learn that nighttime is for sleeping.

Babies can instinctively feel a schedule or routine, and each of you will anticipate the next step if you are consistent.

In these early days, you should not expect your twins to sleep through the night. Your twins will be hungry and eager to feed frequently so that they can keep growing, especially if they were born early or weigh less than 7 pounds. While it is still too soon to expect the miracle of twins sleeping through the night, you should start taking steps from day one to show your babies that daytime is for playing and nighttime is for sleeping. From 8:00 pm or so, through the night until daybreak, keep feeds quiet and efficient. If possible, feed the twins in the room in which they sleep, leaving the lights as low as possible. Only change their diapers if they've had a poop; modern disposable diapers can hold a lot of urine without leaking or causing too much discomfort. After the feeding and burping, cuddle a bit and coax the twins back to sleep. The key is to be as unobtrusive as possible. If a diaper does need to be changed, avoid too much eye contact and communication. The middle of the night is not the time to play or coo with your twins. They should be getting plenty of that during the daytime hours. Now is the time to be quiet and efficient. If you are consistent with your nighttime feeds, even newborns can

> ## *Twin Tip!*
>
> You and your spouse can tag team by alternating overnight feeds so that you each can sleep longer stretches at a time. Dad can handle the midnight feeding (of pumped breast milk or formula) solo, for example; then Mom can handle the 3:00 am feeding solo. This way, each parent can sleep 5 or more hours continuously.

start getting the message that nighttime is for sleeping and daytime is for playing and interacting. I recommend white noise to help infants sleep. A small electric fan in the room can muffle outside noises and signal to the twins that it is sleep time.

⮞ Feeding—Breast Milk or Formula

Every new mother makes a decision whether to breastfeed or formula-feed her babies. The American Academy of Pediatrics encourages breast milk as the optimal nutrition for babies up to 6 months of age, and breastfeeding is strongly encouraged up to 1 year of age (and beyond, if desired). Breastfeeding has many advantages over bottle-feeding. Moms and babies have increased bonding with the physical contact. Breast milk is species-specific for your babies and is easier to digest. Breast milk does not require mixing or preparation, is already at the right temperature, and contains immunologic factors that have been shown to prevent ear infections, diarrhea, and respiratory illnesses. For the mother, nursing helps the uterus contract to its pre-pregnancy state. Breastfeeding moms also burn more calories, which can help facilitate losing the "baby weight." Potentially delayed ovulation and menstruation are another bonus, but do not rely on nursing as a sole form of birth control!

The decision of what to feed is not so easy, however, if you are expecting twins. You may wonder, how on earth can I nurse 2 babies? Will I turn into a human feeding machine? Is it even possible to produce enough milk? Yes, it is very possible to nurse 2 babies.

Twin Tip!

In the first couple of days or so after delivery, you will produce colostrum ("early milk"). These are challenging days to learn to nurse your twins because there is not a lot of volume for your twins to drink. The nursing process becomes simpler once your milk comes in with greater volumes, usually by the fourth or fifth day after delivery. The increased volume of milk helps your twins feel more satisfied after a nursing session.

The removal of breast milk from the milk ducts results in more milk produced for the next feeding. The demand for breast milk creates the supply. Double the demand, and you double the supply. So yes, most mothers should be able to produce enough milk for 2 babies. If you are intimidated by the idea of nursing twins, I suggest some hopeful optimism. Start out by learning how to nurse your twins. See how it goes. Take it a day at a time. For healthy twins in the first week of life, if the babies are still hungry after a nursing session and your milk hasn't really come in yet, supplement with a bit of formula. Supplementing with an ounce or two of formula immediately after your twins have nursed a session at each breast should not inhibit your milk production significantly. Any little bit of colostrum (the early milk) or breast milk the babies ingest is a bonus because it is filled with immunologic factors and other goodies.

Take the breastfeeding experience one week at a time. Ask for help and advice from your pediatrician, and get a referral to a lactation consultant if you need additional resources and support. Try to avoid black-and-white promises to yourself or anyone else that "I will exclusively breastfeed my twins up to 6 months." This is a wonderful goal, and many have done it successfully, but you'll be setting yourself up for extra stress if you decide after 2 months that you need to revisit this decree. The good news is that all infant formula prepared and sold in the United States, whether brand name or store brand, is strictly monitored and contains all the nutritional factors that babies need in the appropriate proportions.

Twin Tip!

Any amount of breast milk your twins receive is beneficial. Do the best you can and ask for support from your pediatrician and lactation consultant as you need it.

I was able to nurse my twins for 3½ months together with some formula supplementation. At that time I made the personal choice, for many reasons, to make the switch to all formula. I will have lifelong wonderful memories of breastfeeding my twin boys on my huge twin-feeding pillow. I also enjoyed the convenience and liberation

I felt when we made the switch to formula, so I've seen both sides of the story. Give breastfeeding a try. See what comes of it. If you go back to formula, that's fine too. Again, any amount of breast milk you can give to your babies is beneficial.

⤜ Breastfeeding—How Do We Do It?

One of the challenges of breastfeeding any number of babies is wondering how much milk the babies are actually taking in. You will learn each of your twin's feeding patterns. One baby may nurse more quickly than the other, finishing up her meal within 10 minutes, while her twin lingers for more than 15 minutes. Babies who are satisfied at the end of a feeding, burp, have good wet diapers, and are stooling at least once a day are, in general, getting enough to eat. By the end of the first week of life your babies should be having about 4 to 6 wet diapers a day and 3 to 6 stools a day. Many breastfed babies stool with every feed; this is normal and happens because breast milk is so easily digested by your babies. Weight checks at the pediatrician's office are the best way to determine if milk intake is adequate.

> ## *Twin Tip!*
> It is likely that one of your twins will be a more vigorous eater than the other. As long as they are both gaining weight appropriately, try to relax and avoid too many comparisons between the two.

Your twins may have 2 different feeding styles, and one twin may be hungrier than the other during a growth spurt. For this reason you may want to remember which baby nursed on which side at each session and then switch sides for the next nursing session. In alternating your twins' nursing sides, you can help even out your milk supply between your left and right breasts so that you don't end up lopsided. In addition, your twins will benefit from lots of experience eating at both sides—babies can at times develop a preference for just one side, and you can curb that tendency by making sure you switch sides often. You need both sides to produce milk evenly.

I had a hard time remembering who nursed on which side when my twins were newborns, so I taped 2 note cards labeled "Andrew" and "Ryan" on the edge of my kitchen island. I would switch the position of the cards according to who nursed on which breast to help me remember to alternate. Even with my note card system, I would forget to alternate a few nursing sessions a day, but when you are nursing 8 to 12 times in 24 hours, it's OK—it all evens out. A good friend of mine wore a plastic bracelet on alternating wrists to indicate on which sides the babies should nurse.

Take notes on your twins' feeding, urinating, and stooling patterns by keeping a simple chart. A chart recording feeding information is helpful in the hospital and in the early days at home. In the chart, include the time of day, the time spent at the breast, whether you supplemented with formula afterward, and whether there was a wet or soiled diaper. Such a chart is an easy way to look at the babies' progress over a 24-hour period; you cannot rely on your memory at this sleep-deprived time in your life! Your pediatrician will want to see this chart when you visit the office in the first week after being discharged from the hospital.

Twin Tip!

For the first couple of weeks, until breastfeeding has been well established, keep a chart to record feeding sessions. Include
- Time of day
- Time spent at the breast
- Any formula volume supplemented afterward
- Wet and soiled diapers

Bring the nursing chart to your appointments with the pediatrician.

The most important indicator of adequate breast milk intake is proper weight gain. In the early days each baby should be gaining at least an ounce a day. This is an important issue that your pediatrician will be following closely with you, especially if your twins were born early or had a low birth weight. Sometimes mothers are concerned that breastfeeding isn't going so well, but the babies' good weight gain bolsters their confidence.

If you are able to pump your breast milk, it is best to store the milk in small increments, no more than 2 or 3 ounces per bottle or freezer bag in the early days. This method prevents waste of any precious breast milk if baby is not especially hungry. If she needs more milk, you can always thaw another serving. Some moms prefer to freeze their breast milk in specially designed plastic bags; other moms stockpile heat- and freezer-safe bottles that attach directly to the breast pump to simplify collection, storage, and feeding.

If you are exclusively nursing your twins, it is important to focus on feeding at the breast as much as possible for the first 3 weeks of life and to avoid pacifier use to prevent nipple confusion. After 3 weeks, you have a special window of opportunity from 3 to 6 weeks of life where breastfed babies more easily learn to feed from a bottle without significantly interfering with feedings at the breast. Take advantage of this opportunity to get your twins accustomed to nursing and bottle-feeding formula or pumped breast milk. Bottle-feeding is a great way for fathers to get involved in the babies' care, promote father-baby bonding, and give mom a break. If you plan on returning to work after a maternity leave you will need to train the twins to accept milk from a bottle and the breast.

How can you train your twins to feed from bottles? Provide dad or another loved one with your twins, bottles of expressed milk, and the twin-feeding pillow. (Warm previously frozen or refrigerated pumped breast milk by floating the lidded bottles in a larger bowl of warm water 10 minutes in advance. Microwaves create dangerous heat pockets and destroy beneficial proteins in breast milk.) The

Twin Tip!

When your twins are 3 to 6 weeks old, you have a window of opportunity to teach them how to feed from the breast and a bottle.

most important step is that you need to physically leave the room! Babies know when mom is around and will prefer her familiar breast to any bottle! Be patient with your twins; it may take a few sessions for them to actually drink anything at all from the bottle. Remember that when a baby really needs milk, she'll drink the milk.

🐤 Formula-Feeding—Simplifying the Process

If you are formula-feeding your twins or even just supplementing nursing with formula, it is useful to make batches of formula at a time. Parents of twins simply do not have the time to prepare powdered formula at every feeding. Purchase 1-quart liquid containers and prepare 2 quarts of formula together to save time. Fill each jug with 30 ounces of formula water, and use a funnel to add 15 scoops of powdered formula (or use the measurements on the side of the can). If you are using concentrated liquid formula, you will mix equal parts concentrate and water. Gently agitate the jug to blend in the powder; warmer water may help the powder blend in more easily. Store the jugs of prepared formula in the refrigerator, and when it's time for the twins to feed, simply pour out the desired ounces into bottles and warm them up. I have found this to be the easiest way to feed 2 hungry babies powdered formula several times a day! Don't forget to use newborn slow-flow nipples to help the babies eat and digest more easily without swallowing excess air.

> ## Twin Tip!
> If you are formula feeding, save time by preparing batches of powdered formula once a day.

Microwaves are a dangerous way to warm bottles because they can create pockets of heat throughout the liquid, and the milk may be a scalding temperature despite feeling relatively cool when held in the hand. The safest way to warm bottles is to float the 2 lidded bottles in a large bowl of warm water in your kitchen sink for about 10 or 15 minutes before the planned feeding time. Anticipate the next feeding ahead of time and get your bottles warming so that they are ready for you when your twins are ready to feed.

The average number of ounces of formula needed per day depends on the babies' weight and age. From birth to 2 months of age, each baby can take anywhere from 2 to 5 ounces per feeding. From 2 to 4 months of age babies usually average 4 to 6 ounces per feed, and from 4 to 6 months of age, 5 to 7 ounces per feed. After 6 months your babies will also be eating solid foods for additional calories, so you really won't need bottles bigger than 7 ounces total. After 12 months healthy babies can transition to whole milk.

If you find a 5- or 6-ounce bottle brand and type that you like, you should stockpile the bottle. Your twins will be formula-feeding every 3 hours on average, which calculates into 16 bottles a day. Decide whether you want to wash bottles frequently or in one big batch once a day. Once your twins are about 1 year old they will be ready to transition to drinking from a cup.

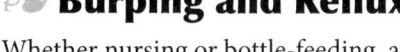 Burping and Reflux

Whether nursing or bottle-feeding, all babies appreciate burp breaks. About halfway through a nursing session, or after each ounce or two of a formula bottle, give your twins some time to burp. Releasing any excess gas that may have gotten caught in the stomach is a good way to help your baby take the rest of the feeding. I have seen many hungry babies inhale a feed quickly, only to spit up a significant portion of the feed because of inhaled air in the stomach! These big spit-ups are not necessarily reflux; often the spit-ups reflect *improper pacing of the feed.* Proper pacing of a feed means giving your babies time to rest and time for any air bubbles in the stomach to rise up and be released before the babies chug the rest of the milk. Even if your twins are ravenously hungry, don't be tempted to feed them too quickly—you'll end up with a huge spit-up in your lap!

Twin Tip!

Generously burp your twins during feeds!

How long do you burp a baby after the feed is complete? Burp your twins until they burp, and then you should burp them some more! It sounds silly, but so many times after the big audible burp, there is a smaller bubble that also needs to come out. At times you may not even hear an audible burp. Not hearing an audible burp is more common if you are breastfeeding, but regardless, make sure you burp each baby at least 5 minutes. Consider the burping time to be cuddle time and enjoy it.

You can burp your twins simultaneously. If you are using a large twin-feeding pillow, you can sit up the twins on either side so that you are hugging and burping both babies at the same time (Figure 3-4). Just make sure you've got a good hold on each of the twins, as their muscle tone is quite weak at this age! Or, you can roll the twins onto their bellies and pat their backs. In this position, make sure to raise your knees so that their heads are inclined up and the milk doesn't come rolling out of their mouths.

Figure 3-4. Burping both babies simultaneously using the twin-feeding pillow.

Twin Tip!

Keep your twins upright for about 20 minutes after each feeding to help them digest their milk more comfortably.

Twins are more likely to be born early, and babies born earlier have a greater chance of developing reflux. Reflux is what its name indicates—milk returning from the stomach, up to the esophagus (the tube that connects the mouth and stomach), and frequently out of the mouth. If your baby spits up frequently but has been gaining weight well, you needn't be too concerned. In this scenario you may want to make sure the baby isn't getting overfed at each feed and is being properly paced with burps midway through the feed. If your baby spits up frequently, is fussy, and is not gaining weight as well as your pediatrician may like, reflux may be the culprit. If you are formula feeding your doctor may switch formulas or prescribe a medication depending on the baby and situation.

After each feeding and burping is complete, try not to lay the baby flat immediately afterward. Imagine eating a big holiday meal and then laying flat—you would feel pretty uncomfortable. Place your twins in bouncy chairs with a 45-degree upright angle, or even wear one of the babies in a front-pack carrier. This way your twins can look around and let the milk settle in their stomach.

⪻ Advice for Outings

For the first 3 weeks that your twins are home with you, I recommend that they lay low and stay at home. I advise this even if your twins were born full term and healthy. All newborns' immune systems are quite immature. There are a lot of cooties out in the world! Little old ladies at the mall will spy your teeny twins and won't be able to restrain themselves from reaching out to make physical contact. You have enough on your plate without your twin newborns catching a virus! So wait a couple of weeks before you take the twins on an outing, and when you are out and about, be straightforward and direct with overly friendly and curious strangers. They can look, but they can't touch! A simple, "Please don't touch my babies, they're getting over a cold," should fend away curiosity. Make sure visitors in your home wash their hands with soap and water before holding your new babies.

> ## *Twin Tip!*
> There is an outside world out there! Whether you leave your babies with a trusted adult or take them with you, after about 3 weeks be sure to get out there to maintain some perspective.

Once your twins are older than 3 weeks, getting out of the house periodically is a nice way to keep your sanity. Staring at the same walls of one's home attending to the needs of 2 very high-maintenance little creatures without an occasional glimpse of the outside world is not healthy. A simple neighborhood walk will give everyone some fresh air. Even a car trip to the drive-through post office mailbox can be a hoot if you are desperate to get out of the house! In case inspiration or necessity strikes, be ready for an outing in advance.

A stocked, ready-to-go diaper bag makes it easier to be spontaneous and take the twins out of the house. You'll have a better chance of going out if your diaper bag is ready to go. In your diaper bag, keep a plastic food storage bag with baby bottles filled with formula water, some packets of powdered formula (the kind that are premeasured—no scoop necessary), and disposable nipples. These ingredients will allow you to easily shake up a tasty meal for the twins while on the road. Of course toss in diapers, wipes, and other necessary items. After an outing, try to restock your bag when you get a chance so that you're ready for the next trip.

If space permits, consider storing your twin stroller in the car trunk so that it is ready to go too. You won't have to lug it to load it each time you need it to run an errand. It's all about simplification! If you have an older toddler, consider placing him in the twin stroller with one twin and carrying the other twin in a soft front-pack carrier. With this technique you won't have to chase after a runaway toddler; everyone is contained and safe. It may be simpler to pop the twins' infant car safety seats into the stroller if yours permits.

Twin Tip!

Store extra emergency baby supplies in your car so you're ready for anything.

In addition to your usual diaper bag, keep a special bag designated to stay in your car in case of emergency. Usually the hospital or your pediatrician's office has plenty of freebie diaper bags that are great for this purpose. In this bag, toss a couple of bottles of formula water, premeasured packets of powdered formula, extra diapers and wipes, changes of clothes, and some receiving blankets. This bag is meant to carry extras of your twins' necessities, just in case. The emergency stash of supplies is good for peace of mind in case you ever get a flat tire while driving with your twins, for example. It is also convenient if you're making a quick trip to run an errand and don't feel like checking the status of your usual diaper bag. You know that if your trip runs longer than you expect, you've got supplies on hand if needed. Anything that helps you get out of the house more frequently will be good for your and your twins' sanity—a very healthy thing indeed.

Infant Colic Times 2

And speaking of sanity…colicky babies have been known to endanger the very existence of one's sanity. What does the word *colic* mean, exactly? It is an older term that many people still use today to describe a young infant's tendency to be fussy. In the past, most people believed that a lot of baby crying and fussiness was caused by gas pains. The current thinking is that there is a spectrum of "infantile fussiness" (my preferred term) that may or may not be related to any gas pains. All babies are fussy at various times and to various degrees.

One of your twins may cry more than the other, depending on each individual baby's temperament. Try not to compare your babies, and don't feel guilty if you find yourself annoyed with one twin who cries more than the other. Parents of twins often feel guilty about carrying the fussier twin more often. Do your best to fairly distribute cuddles to both your babies, whether fussy or calm. You're looking to be *fair* to your 2 babies; it is impossible to give them perfectly *equal* experiences.

Infant crying tends to peak in intensity around 6 weeks and is typically vastly improved by 3 months of age. Any time that one or both of your twins are fussy or crying, make it your routine to run down a mental list of potential triggers.

- Is the baby hungry?
- Does the baby need more burping?
- Is the baby's diaper dirty or wet?
- Is the baby cold, hot, or in pain?
- Does the baby need to be swaddled (to mimic the close environment of the womb)?

- Is the baby tired? Look at the clock. Has the baby been awake more than an hour and a half?
- Does the baby need to suck? Show your baby his or her hand and thumb, or use a pacifier if you prefer.

   If your baby is still crying after addressing all of these issues, she is probably having a colicky moment. You may notice that late afternoon and dinnertime are particularly noisy at your house. Babies fuss more commonly during these times, in theory because the baby is worn out from all the exciting activity and stimulation during the day. Often the crying can occur a total of 3 hours a day several times a week.

   Because we cannot have conversations with newborns, no one knows exactly why they sometimes cry for no apparent reason. Studies have shown that the crying of colic does not seem to be related to pain. Rather, it seems to be related to a heightened sensitivity to the environment surrounding the baby. Imagine if you had been living in a cuddly, warm womb for months and were now suddenly expected to live out in the open, noisy, chaotic world. Minor sounds are like nails on a chalkboard to you, thus causing you to cry your heart out.

   Colic does seem to have one positive benefit—it can assist parent-baby bonding, as holding a crying baby close usually helps her to calm down. Some have theorized that improved bonding is an evolutionary advantage of colic. Human babies, compared with most other animal species' babies, are very dependent on their parents for their care and survival. Over thousands of years, parents' ears and brains have been hardwired to respond to the sound of their babies crying, resulting in the babies surviving and growing. So even though your twins' crying may drive you crazy at times, the crying does serve a purpose. It ensures that you and your twin babies will get lots of hugs every day!

   We do know that all babies of all cultures and ethnicities are affected by colic to varying degrees. We also know that the severity of colic has no correlation to future behavior and development. If one or both of your twins has colic, he still has just as good a chance as any other "calm" baby to develop into a normal grade-schooler, teenager, and adult. Don't worry that your screaming

5-week-old will stay that way forever. He will grow out of it with no harmful effects.

> ## *Twin Tip!*
> One twin is usually more "high maintenance" than the other. Don't worry that you are neglecting the calmer twin. Relax—you may hold one twin more than the other some days, but over the months and years it will all even out. In the long run, each of your twins will need more of you at different times.

Because the crying can be related to the stimuli around your babies, simulating the comforting womb environment results in more effective soothing techniques. Swaddle your twins well to mimic the tight uterine space. Walk with the babies in front-pack carriers to mimic the swaying in the womb. Rock your twins. A humming fan or even static on an AM radio can create helpful white noise. Your womb had a constant hum of activity—imagine your babies in your uterus, with your aorta rhythmically swooshing near their heads. Although it seems counterintuitive, absolute silence can be new and upsetting to a newborn's ears.

If you are at your limit listening to the cries of your twins, you need to take a break. Enlist your spouse, a relative, or a friend to cuddle with the twins while you take a walk or a shower. Even an hour's break will help you survive this challenging period. Absolutely never shake a baby in frustration—this could cause irreversible harm to your baby. It is OK to put a crying baby down in a safe spot such as a crib, close the door, and give yourself a break if you are at your wit's end. Remember, your twins will outgrow the crying!

❧ Should We Use Pacifiers?

Whether to use pacifiers is something that every set of parents must decide for themselves. Many parents happily and successfully use pacifiers, do not regret their decision, and would use them again. Recent studies have shown that a pacifier can lessen the risk of sudden infant death syndrome. However, I would argue that in the world of twins, parents need to simplify their lives. Pacifiers need to be kept clean and available for newborns to satisfy their need for nonnutritive sucking.

Consider simplifying your life and going without pacifiers. The upshot of the pacifier-free life is that your twins will find a way to soothe themselves. There are 2 of them and 1 of you, and you don't need to hear them crying for you when they can't find their dropped pacifier during a night awakening. Without pacifiers, your twins will find their thumbs and comfort themselves back to sleep while you're catching up on much-needed sleep. Anything that helps your twins become more independent and self-reliant will help you as a parent. However, if your twins are quite fussy and nothing else seems to help, certainly go ahead and use pacifiers.

Twin Tip!

In the first weeks of life, twins are very dependent on their parents. But throughout your twins' early months and years, encourage self-reliance. Your twins will be empowered by learning to soothe themselves.

🐦 Seeking Support

Ask, ask, and ask everyone for help. Try to accept everyone's offers for help. Now is not the time to be proud and try to handle everything on your own. Delegate specific tasks, like picking up a gallon of milk at the store. Well-intentioned friends and family cannot imagine what you're going through, unless they have twins themselves, and may not be able to guess what it is that you need. If anyone happens to offer, "If you need help, let me know," *do* take them up on it. Because they do not know what you need, be specific in what you ask of them. Picking up diapers at the store, dropping off a casserole dinner, or playing with the babies for 20 minutes so that you can shower are all good, specific things that won't be difficult for your friend to do and would make such a positive difference

> ## *Twin Tip!*
> Don't underestimate the kindness of strangers! Look beyond family and friends to neighbors and your place of worship for support. Many congregations regularly organize meal delivery volunteers to help member families with newborns at home.

for you. When loved ones ask, "Is there anything we can do to help?" be ready with a specific request.

Depending on your level of comfort and closeness, you can also ask for assistance with overnight awakenings and feedings. Just one night of 6 hours of uninterrupted sleep will help you function much better. My dearest childhood friend visited us from out of state and offered to get up with the babies overnight so that I could sleep. I hadn't even taken her up on the suggestion, but already I felt such a wave of relief knowing that her help was available. When struggling through difficult times, it is important psychologically to know that you have help should you need it.

It is a good idea to make sure that there is a second trusted adult in your nearby geographic area who is available to help in case one twin gets sick and needs medical attention. If your partner goes out of town on business, this person can be on call to stay home with your other twin and children should you need urgent medical care for one twin or child. Hopefully you will never need to use this backup, but you don't want to be caught unprepared should something happen.

Going to the Pediatrician

Plan in advance to have an extra pair of hands with you when you bring your twins to the pediatrician for both well checkups and sick visits, whether it is your spouse, a family member, or a friend. You will invariably have questions about each of your twins. Write your questions down on note cards in advance so that you don't forget them. Have your helper hold one baby while you speak with your doctor about the baby currently being examined. You don't want to be distracted by managing both babies at once—no one can ask important questions this way.

Make sure your pediatrician treats your twins as individuals and gives you an opportunity to discuss one child at length before switching gears to the twin. You may have some global questions that involve both twins, but you will need time to discuss each twin independently and have your questions about that specific twin addressed.

Twin Tip!

Your twins will visit the pediatrician many times in their early months of life. Plan ahead to bring a second adult to each visit. If one twin needs a sick visit, leave the healthy twin at home with a trusted adult while you bring the affected twin to the pediatrician, one-on-one.

Getting Into a Routine

After your twins' first 2 or 3 months, you'll start to see that things are settling into more of a routine and less of a chaotic mess. By now, however, you have 8 weeks or so of poor sleep piling up and the exhaustion may be starting to take its toll. Your twins are going to reward you around this time with glimmers of their first social smiles. Suddenly, all the sleep deprivation and chaos is worth it to see these 2 little babies smiling at you! Enjoy it and pat yourself on the back—you've earned these smiles! Now things are really going to get more fun and interesting with each passing month. The twins are becoming more aware of the world around them and are ready to interact more with you and each other. Now that you have learned the fundamentals of caring for your twins, you're ready to relax a bit and enjoy the beautiful moments of your twin journey!

Early Infancy and Getting on a Schedule

Congratulations! You have survived the first couple of months with your twins! Give yourself a pat on the back—you deserve it! Remind yourself frequently that the toughest days are likely behind you. With every passing week, you and your babies are getting to know each other more and more. Your babies are gaining weight each day and becoming stronger. You are learning the best ways to soothe them. They are learning to trust in you and your loving care. Your twins are comforted by the sight and smell of you. Your twins have grown to be aware of and anticipate your consistent love and responses on a very primary and basic level.

Your household routine is growing more regular and consistent. A consistent home routine will simplify your life and your care of the twins. On a regular schedule, your twins will know what to expect, and they will be more calm in general. A regular schedule benefits you as a parent as well. You will know what your twins will need at what times—whether it be a bottle of milk, more burping, or a nap.

What do young infants do all day? Sleep and eat! Your twins' basic needs of milk and sleep are more easily handled with a consistent schedule. When parents of twins synchronize these 2 basic needs, there is more free time each day to enjoy the babies. You will run yourself ragged if your babies nap on different schedules and are fed separately. You will have more energy and be a much better, more effective parent with synchronized daily schedules.

Sleep—Infant Twins (and Parents) Need It!

Around the 2-month mark, your twins may be sleeping for longer stretches at a time, but as parents, your energy levels are probably dipping. At this point during the early infancy months, parents of twins can feel as if they are running in the second half of a marathon. The end of the pregnancy was tiring enough, between a huge belly and the inability to get comfortable or a good night's rest. Now you have weeks upon weeks of sleep-deprived nights piling up.

> ## *Twin Tip!*
> Be proactive—teach your twins good sleep habits now.
> The benefits of good sleep are well worth the effort!

During all the feedings and diaper changes, it is also challenging to find time for a break to rejuvenate and reenergize as a parent.

All of the sleep deprivation and stress can start to have a cumulative effect. Sleep deprivation affects all areas of a family's life. If mom and dad don't get enough sleep, tensions run higher, coping with routine household and relationship issues becomes more difficult, and everyone is cranky. Don't worry—there is a light at the end of the tunnel! Parents of twins can be proactive to help their children soothe themselves to sleep. A well-rested baby is a happier baby, and a well-rested parent is a more effective parent!

I'll never forget when my eldest, single-born son was 2 months old and the sleepless nights were starting to take their toll on my husband and me—and it was only *one* baby waking up! A friend reassured us, "Oh, don't worry, my daughter started to sleep through the night when she was 9 months old." She thought she was putting our minds at ease, but the only thing I could think was, "There is *no way* I can keep living like this for 7 more months!" A healthy, otherwise normal baby can sleep through the night sooner than 9 months of age.

How much sleep do babies need in early infancy? On average, 2- to 3-month-old babies need 15 hours of sleep in a 24-hour period. About 9 or 10 of the 15 hours of sleep should be nighttime sleep, and the remaining 5 or so hours should be divided into 3 daytime naps. Babies can start transitioning to a 2-nap-a-day schedule around the time they are 6 months old.

Parents need to make sure that they are not encouraging or prolonging sleep problems by dealing with overnight awakenings incorrectly. Do you enter your babies' room at 2:00 am, turn on some bright lights, and start smiling and cooing to your twins? If you do, you've got some changes to make!

The good news is that most babies can learn to sleep through the night, meaning more than 6 to 8 hours in a stretch, by the time they are 3 months old and weigh more than 12 pounds. When a baby reaches 12 pounds, his stomach capacity is large enough that overnight feedings are no longer required. All of the baby's daily calories and nutrition can and should be taken during the daytime hours. With less frequent feedings at night, the baby can sleep for longer stretches. If you are breastfeeding, your body will adjust to the changing overnight feeding schedule.

Twin Tip!

If your twins were born early or small, they will need overnight feedings a bit longer than a full-term baby would. Once your babies are more than 12 pounds, though, you can confidently proceed with sleep training.

⚶ Two Cribs or 2 Bedrooms?

If your twins share a bedroom, are they still sharing a crib? In the early days after coming home from the hospital, many twin newborns are comforted by their twin's presence nearby. As they get bigger and squirmier, though, they will need their own crib space. Having 2 cribs for your twins ensures that they have the space that they need to comfort themselves to sleep. A borrowed crib that meets national safety standards fits the budget perfectly! You will be especially pleased when time flies and it is time to transition to a big-kid bed. You'll be so glad that you saved the money.

Will it be more difficult to sleep train your twin babies if they share a bedroom? I don't think so. Your babies become accustomed to their bedroom environment, and they accept the presence of their twin as part of the environment of the room. Most parents of twins have their twin babies share a bedroom because of space restraints in the home. Don't worry about the shared room interfering with the twins' learning process to sleep on their own.

It has always amazed me how twins have a way of blocking out their twin's noises. Many a time I walked into my twin babies' bedroom while one boy was screaming his head off and the other was sleeping as peacefully as could be. It boggled my mind! Somehow twins can shut out such overnight noises from their twin, and this skill will extend into the preschool years. You do not need to buy a bigger home with more bedrooms to get your twins to sleep through the night.

🐚 The Science Behind Good Sleep Habits

During overnight sleep, all humans transition through various sleep stages. During these normal transitional episodes, sleep may be interrupted. Even as adults, we may not always be aware of it, but we have various points throughout the night where we are more awake than others because we are transitioning through the various sleep stages. When we briefly awaken between sleep stages, and we are in our familiar bed at our home, we can just get ourselves back to sleep quite easily. However, if we are in an unfamiliar place, it can take longer to fall back asleep.

Twin Tip!

During the process of sleep training your twins, it will be important to recognize which of your twins' overnight awakenings are from *hunger* and which are a normal *awakening period* between sleep stages in which they are trying to fall asleep once again. Are your twins crying at 2:00 am? Do they weigh more than 12 pounds? If yes, don't assume the babies are hungry and automatically feed them. Give them a chance to settle themselves back to sleep.

One analogy to this phenomenon is traveling away from home—if you are sleeping in a hotel room and you wake up at 2:00 am with an unfamiliar pillow under your head, you may not be able to fall asleep again as quickly as usual because conditions are slightly different from those at your home. Your twins' ability to fall asleep can be affected by a change in routine the same way. If a parent is always present when the baby falls asleep, that baby won't be able to fall asleep without the parent! Therefore, your babies should learn from an early age how to fall asleep *without a parent present*.

The time that your babies are falling asleep is the moment in which they need to be in a familiar setting, in conditions in which they have fallen asleep before. If a parent is always immediately rushing in to comfort the child, that child will require the parent's presence to fall asleep once again. If your twins are always rocked to sleep, they won't be able to fall asleep without the familiar rocking routine. If your twins always fall asleep when nursing or taking a bottle, they won't be able to put themselves to sleep without drinking milk. Give your twins lots of practice falling asleep on their own at 7:00 or 8:00 pm, and your children will be able to get themselves back to sleep on their own if they wake up between sleep cycles at 2:00 am.

A special note—if your twins were born *small or premature*, they may still require overnight feedings at 2 and 3 months of age. But even if your twins still require the overnight feeds, use the following strategies to help them fall back asleep by themselves. As your twins gain more weight, they will be better sleepers.

Twin Tip!

When a parent is faced with 2 tired, fussy babies, it is human nature to want to hold and rock the babies until they fall asleep. It is hard-wired into our brains to actively help a wailing baby. Unfortunately, if your twins are always rocked to sleep, in the long run, they will not be able to fall asleep without the rocking.

ew Strategies for Good Sleep Habits

There are 2 key strategies that will help your twins learn to sleep through the night. The first strategy is a good daily schedule and routine. Daytime should be filled with lots of play, interaction, and consistency. The second and perhaps more important strategy is that your twins have plenty of practice putting themselves to sleep on their own. Over time, your twins will learn that daytime is for eating, playing, and interacting, and nighttime is for sleeping. When your babies are placed in their cribs *awake* at bedtime, they learn how to fall asleep on their own. Then if they wake up again at 2:00 am, they know what to do—go right back to sleep, without bothering mom, dad, or their twin!

Twin Tip!

No matter how old your twins are or what they weigh, from 8:00 pm to 7:00 am, be as boring as possible! Leave the lights low and keep the white noise humming!

During the overnight hours, keep the bedroom lights as low as possible, even if your twins wake up for a feeding. Try to handle the awakening by night light only, and only turn on a soft light if you need help changing a poopy diaper. I put a 25-watt light bulb in our twins' bedroom lamp so that diaper changes would not be lit too brightly. If your babies have stooled, quietly change their diapers, but otherwise, let the diaper be. A diaper change with all the undressing and air exposure wakes babies from their sleepy state, making it more difficult to settle back to sleep. Modern disposable diapers are strong enough to hold several hours of overnight urine comfortably. Keep your facial expressions as close to a poker face as you can—now is not the time for eye contact, cooing to your twins, or rousing renditions of "The Itsy-Bitsy Spider." Your twins should be getting plenty of fun and games in the daytime.

Keep sending the message that daytime is for playing and night-time is for sleeping. In the night, when your babies realize they won't be getting much more out of you than a feeding and a burping, they have no choice but to fall asleep. If your twins weigh more than 12 pounds each, they should not get any overnight milk from you.

If just one of your twins is still underweight, however, go ahead and quietly and efficiently feed her as unobtrusively as you can, then leave the room again. If you are concerned that her twin will get

Twin Tip!

Good sleep habits are important for any young child and are especially critical for families with twins or more. Avail yourself of additional sleep resources if need be. *Healthy Sleep Habits, Happy Twins* by Marc Weissbluth, MD, FAAP, has advice specific for the needs of families with multiples. *Solve Your Child's Sleep Problems* by Richard Ferber, MD, FAAP, is filled with excellent sleep advice as well. Children who are good sleepers are happy, healthy children!

jealous, you can quickly feed her in a second, darkened, quiet room before returning her to her bedroom.

It is really challenging to sleep train just 1 baby, let alone 2. But do not procrastinate—the longer sleep training is delayed, the more difficult the overall process will be. As your infants grow, they will begin to develop *object permanence,* meaning that they will know you exist even when you leave the room and are not in their direct sight. If your twins are 9 months old and aware that you are outside their closed door, sleep training will be that much more difficult! Sleep training is also more challenging if your twins are already sitting up or pulling to a stand. It is preferable to sleep train at an earlier age when your babies are more adaptable.

Twin Tip!

Good sleep habits can be temporarily interrupted by illness or travel. You will need to tend to your babies in the overnight hours if they are feverish or coughing. When everyone is healthy once again, you may need to retrain your babies to sleep through the night. If they had previously been sleeping through the night before the illness or travel, they will remember quickly.

ॐ The Power of the Bedtime Ritual

Your twins' early infancy months are a good time to initiate a consistent evening ritual. The beauty of the ritual is that if you do it every evening, it will cue your twins that it will soon be time for sleep. If you are consistent with a bedtime routine, you will be richly rewarded in the following several years with children who easily go to bed at a healthy hour.

Of course, there will be occasional times that you cannot stick to the usual nighttime routine. Sometimes you will have a date night with your spouse, and your babysitting relatives may do things a bit differently. There will be times when you'll all be out late for some fun event, and that's OK. But for the most part, do your best to keep your evening rituals as consistent as possible.

Twin Tip!

A calm, relaxing bedtime routine sets the tone for a good overnight sleep.

Our family has enjoyed the benefits of a bedtime routine for years. Thanks to our evening ritual, for the most part our kids have turned in for the night quite easily with minimal conflict or fuss. An added bonus is that my husband and I have wonderful grown-up evenings to catch up with each other and to do whatever else we need to do.

Our bedtime routine starts with a good tooth-brushing session, or in the pre-toothed set, using a clean, wet washcloth to rub the gums. Next comes a quick splash in the bathtub, and I do mean quick. Yes, we give nightly baths, but if it is not summertime and your kid is not particularly stinky or dirty, we are talking about a quickie wash of the face, hands, feet, and lastly the private parts. Three-month-olds are not crawling around the house picking up dust balls. Thus, you know you can give a quick and effective bath, all the while letting your twins explore the water, learn to splash, and have some fun!

At bath time in the first 6 months of life, our twins couldn't sit up unsupported yet. We would use an infant bathtub and bathe the boys one at a time in succession. Save some time, water, and energy by using the same bathwater for both twins, assuming that everyone is generally healthy. After the first twin is plucked out of the tub and handed off to your partner, grab a new washcloth and get the second twin in the tub.

After the baths comes pajama time, and then our favorite, story time. One parent can read to one twin while the other parent reads to the second twin. Alternatively, one parent can read to both twins at the same time. How can you read to 2 kids at once when your young babies don't have the muscle tone to really sit by themselves yet? Get creative. One way is to sit them up in a comfy reading chair together and sit on the floor in front of them. Face them so they don't fall, and hold the book up in front of them as you read. If your spouse or other adult can help you, have your helper place one child on each of your thighs in your lap, and you can snuggle and support them as you read. As you read books with your infant twins, they may not understand the words or images that they see in the books yet, but hearing the rhythm and sound of your voice is soothing. Over time, your twins will start to realize that the images in the books represent real-life things. It is never too early to start reading to your babies!

After reading time is finished, some extra cuddling and a little lullaby song with the lights turned off helps to transition your twins to sleep. Then the fan is turned on, the twins are laid in their cribs *while still awake,* and the door is closed. They may be awake for the next 30 minutes, but these 30 minutes are when they'll figure out how to put themselves to sleep.

If your twins cry after you leave the room and cannot settle themselves down, you can periodically check on them to reassure them and make sure they are safe; but after you check on them, lay them down awake in their cribs and leave the room once again. If they can convince you to rock them to sleep one more time, they'll always try to get you to do so. Babies should be left alone in their cribs for increasing stretches of time, with parents periodically checking on them and reassuring them, until they learn to finally fall asleep on their own.

Twin Tip!

What if one parent works late some nights or all nights? You don't want your babies to miss seeing the working parent too many nights. You'll have to work out a system that works for your family. Perhaps you can compromise a couple of nights a week, giving your twins an extra-late nap before dinnertime so that they can spend some quality time with the late-working parent when he or she gets home.

Some of your friends or relatives may question your adherence to a consistent bedtime ritual. Starting good sleep habits now will extend into the next several years. Maybe your friend has only one kid and has no problem taking care of a cranky toddler at 9:30 at night asking for more water; but with twins, you don't have time for that sort of thing! When you have multiples in your family, you've got to do what it takes to help them go to sleep easily. Your children will be happy and healthy because they are *well rested.*

Twin Tip!

The quality and quantity of your twins' sleep is of vital importance to your family. With good sleep habits, your twins will be happier and healthier. Good sleep boosts each baby's immune system to fend off illness more effectively. And if your babies sleep well, you will have extra time in your day to take care of yourself and all the household tasks! If you haven't quite reached this point yet, hang in there—your current efforts and strategies will ultimately pay off!

🐋 Daytime Naps

During the daytime, remember to keep your twins' schedules coordinated with synchronized sleeping, eating, burping, playing, diaper changes, then more sleep. As mentioned in the previous chapter, babies can only tolerate being awake during the day for a couple of hours. So watch the clock from the time your twins wake up from their nap. Of course, if both twins are not waking up at the same time, you'll need to wake up your second baby so that you can keep the 2 babies on the same schedule.

When your twins have fed, burped, played, and had tummy time, you will probably star to notice some signs of fatigue. Your babies' signs of fatigue will show you when you should scoop them up and initiate the pre-nap routine. This sends the message that sleep is coming. For your routine, you can read the babies a story, give them fresh diapers, dress them in sleepers if you use them, and lay them down in their cribs in their darkened room. At this point, they are resting in their cribs in their darkened room, and they are fatigued, fed, clean, and content. What else is there to do but close one's eyes and sleep? This is the time when the twins will get practice falling asleep on their own, with their twin doing the same in the other crib across the room.

Twin Tip!

Remember that crying is a late sign of fatigue. Look for earlier clues that your twins are sleepy, such as thumb sucking or rubbing their eyes or ears.

🐋 Feeding Your Infant Twins

If you are still able to nurse your twins at this point, good for you! You may be supplementing with formula, which is perfectly fine. Any amount of breast milk your twins can get from you will be beneficial. For our family, daytime nursing with a supplemental evening bottle of formula helped my twins sleep better through the night. The formula "tanked them up," so to speak, and they didn't get as hungry overnight. We referred to their evening formula bottles as their milkshakes that tucked them in for the night!

If your twins are feeding well and not having trouble with spit-ups or reflux, you may consider advancing the nipple speed that you use with your bottles. Many nipple manufacturers make a slow-flow nipple with a small hole for newborns, followed by a medium-flow nipple, and a fast-flow nipple with the largest opening. If your twins are handling feeds well, experiment with a larger nipple opening. If you can safely use a faster nipple speed without causing excessive gas or spit-ups, you can shorten the duration of a milk feeding by 5 minutes. If you can save 5 minutes in each of the 5 feedings a day, you will have 25 extra minutes in your busy day. Simple time-saving tricks can help your life with twins get easier each month!

Your twins will not need additional solid foods with the breast milk or formula until they are 4 to 6 months of age. The amount of milk they drink at each feeding will increase as they grow. Their daily intake of milk should be about 30 ounces by 4 months of age, divided over about 5 feedings a day. Again, mixing the batches of formula ahead of time in quart-sized jugs will continue to simplify the process of readying 2 bottles of milk for each feeding.

At 4 months of age you can start to feed your twins solid foods such as infant cereals as well as pureed and strained vegetables and fruits. Do not be tempted to add infant cereal to the milk bottles to help them sleep through the night—it doesn't work and may lead to excessive weight gain. The way to help your twins sleep all night is by encouraging good sleep habits as previously discussed.

You will need 2 high chairs to feed your twins solid foods. High chairs have a wide range of prices. The safety seats that strap into existing kitchen chairs with an infant seat belt and eating tray work well and are also budget friendly. In keeping with a consistent schedule for your twins, feed your twins solid foods at the same time and place. Place their high chairs close together, in front of you, at a 90-degree angle to one another so that they can see each other as well as you (Figure 4-1). Mealtimes can be a fun bonding time for all of you. Make sure to introduce only one new food at a time, waiting 3 days or so before introducing another new food to ensure that your twins do not have a reaction to the food. Store-bought

baby food is just fine;
the pureed pears are
particularly delicious. If
you have lots of energy
you can also prepare food
in advance by pureeing,
straining, and freezing
the food in ice cube trays,
later popping the cubes
of food out and repackag-
ing in resealable storage
bags for safe storage.
Do what works for
your family.

Figure 4-1. High chairs at 90 degrees from one another so the caregiver can feed both babies while creating a nice three-way social experience at the same time.

Twin Tip!

Do not be surprised when you discover your infant twins have different taste preferences. They are 2 unique individuals! If one child is resisting a certain food, do not write off that particular food forever. Keep offering it, and over time your babies will accept it and broaden their palates' horizons.

Teaching 2 babies to eat solid foods can get quite messy. In the early days, feeding solid foods once a day is a nice way to slowly introduce the concept. As your twins' skills in eating pureed foods from an offered spoon improve, you can increase the solid feeds over the next several weeks to twice a day, then to 3 times a day.

Twin Tip!

Get your camera ready! Two babies learning how to eat solid foods is a real photo opportunity!

ᴓ Twins Getting Stronger

At 2 and 3 months of age, your twins are starting to develop their muscle tone. Their upper trunks and neck muscles are strengthening, and when placed on the floor prone they are able to start lifting their heads on their own. It is our job as parents to become at-home physical therapists and to make sure we give our twins plenty of practice strengthening their muscles.

Tummy time will help your babies gain strength as well as protect their heads from developing plagiocephaly, or a flattening of a part of the skull that can partly result from frequently laying on one's back. The Back to Sleep campaign has been invaluable in educating families about proper sleep positioning to minimize the risk of sudden infant death syndrome, but babies also need plenty of practice holding their bodies in other positions when they are awake and supervised.

> ### *Twin Tip!*
> Twins outnumber their mom or dad—they can't be held simultaneously all day. As a result, parents of twins love the convenience of bouncy chairs, swings, and the like to entertain and contain our babies. Make sure to avoid overuse of such devices. Playtime on the open floor will help your twins develop their muscles and strength.

In the early stages, tummy time can be frustrating for babies and parents alike. Your babies may just cry and fuss immediately, unable to budge their heavy heads up. Tummy time works best if you can give your babies something interesting to look at while on their tummies. It is an advantage to have 2 babies because your twins can face each other with baby toys between them. A mirror

Figure 4-2. Tummy time fun!

to look into is another popular option, but one's own twin can be just as interesting! For comfort's sake, you can position a regular throw or Boppy pillow under the upper chest (Figure 4-2). It gives your twins a slightly higher and more interesting vantage point and if their head droops suddenly, the fall is cushioned.

Always supervise tummy time directly. Even if tummy time lasts only 2 minutes and you have to end it because of tears, every minute counts. Try to incorporate tummy time into your daily routine of playing and eating. After the feed and burp is a good time for tummy time. You can perform tummy time on mom or dad's chest as well. Your goal is to give your twins tummy time several times throughout each day.

When you have twins, a parent can come to love bouncy chairs. It is quite a luxury to have the option of keeping your twins safe and comfortable while you tend to things around the house. A word of caution, however—parents of multiples need to make sure that they do not overuse such containment receptacles. It will be difficult for your babies to practice using their muscles if they are strapped and confined in bouncy seats too often. You can briefly use the luxury of your bouncy chairs after a feed, for example, as the 45-degree incline can help your babies digest their milk, but after you have rinsed out the bottles and put away the jug of formula, pick your babies up and give them time on the open floor.

Babies usually start to roll over around 4 months of age. That being said, rolling for the first time could easily happen earlier, surprising you and your child! Because you never know when your twin babies will start to roll over, never *ever* leave them unattended in high places such as a bed, couch, or changing table. Consider changing your twins' wet diapers right there on the carpet floor where you are all playing already. If there is no poop in the diaper, save yourself the trip to the changing table where your attention becomes divided between the baby on the table and the baby on the floor. Accidents are more likely to happen when a parent is distracted. You will get very speedy and efficient with diaper changes, trust me!

After the first month of life, your babies learn to visually track and follow you and other objects. They will hear you coming from the next room and turn their heads to your voice. These new skills

> ## *Twin Tip!*
> Ah, such is the life of a parent of twins—your attention is divided between your babies! Never leave either of your babies in a high position from which they can roll off. You will be busy tending to her twin and won't be able to intervene in time!

will help them form relationships and interact with the world around them!

Once the twins are 4 months old, everything seems to be getting a little bit easier. The babies are getting better at amusing themselves and each other for increasing amounts of time. Most babies also begin sleeping through the night by 3 months of age and 12 pounds in weight. Solid feeds may have begun and give more structure to the day's activities. Four to 6 months is a time for you to step back, look at how far you and your twins have come, and enjoy the relative ease of these days compared with those chaotic early weeks.

🐌 Diaper Rash

Diaper rash is common among babies after introducing solid foods to their diet. As a parent of twins, you do not have time for diaper rash! Learn how to banish it quickly so that you can all move on with your lives. Be aware of the relationship between solid foods and diaper rash—some preventive care can help keep diaper rash at bay. The warm, moist environment within a diaper triggers diaper rash; unfortunately, modern diapers are excellent at retaining moisture. When changing diapers, do not rush to put the new diaper on so quickly. Give your babies' bottoms some air time, or diaper-free time, just for a couple of minutes to truly dry out the skin usually closed up in a diaper.

If you have a case or two of diaper rash in your house, start using a zinc oxide–containing cream with each diaper change. Make sure you are *generous* with the cream. Use the cream like frosting on a cake—you need a bit more than you think. The zinc oxide cream is a barrier cream. There are many zinc oxide–containing creams on the market, all of which work pretty well. My personal favorite brand adds cornstarch to the zinc oxide mix, which together seems to really zap the rash quickly. I would also suggest avoiding the use of commercial baby wipes to clean soiled skin when your baby has an active diaper rash. Even the wipes labeled "For sensitive skin" contain irritating chemicals, so consider temporarily replacing wipes with 100% cotton balls dipped in a bowl of warm water to clean the skin during diaper rash.

Another strategy to eliminate diaper rash is to increase your babies' air time between diaper changes. One trick I used when my twins were babies was to have a few pairs of casual, comfy, all-cotton pants on hand as extras, specifically to put on my boys when they were getting air time. The sweatpants helped catch some spills if the boys happened to pee during air time—warning, exposure to the air tends to stimulate urination!

Another trick I used when my boys had diaper rash was to combine air time with tummy time using waterproof pads. A strategically-placed waterproof pad makes it possible to combine tummy-air time and catch any accidental urination that could occur without a diaper. Parents of twins learn to be quite efficient, and you too will learn how to multitask this way. Healing up a diaper rash and encouraging upper body strength at the same time is just one example of how you can streamline your life with twins!

Certainly, if a diaper rash is not clearing up as quickly as you'd like or if it looks particularly worrisome, have your pediatrician check it out. Some diaper rashes can progress to a yeast infection of the skin, which requires a prescription medication for treatment.

﹅ Twinproofing

Now that the babies are starting to move more and roll over, it is a good time to start intensively childproofing your home. Parents of twins should be extra vigilant and perform *twinproofing* of their home because twins have a way of giving each other ideas. Twins also help each other to get into restricted areas that one baby alone could not have ventured into by herself. Some ideas to help you get started with twinproofing your home include

- Safety gates for the top and bottom of staircases
- Doorknob covers
- Electric outlet covers
- Window blind cords secured out of reach
- All nursery furniture far from windows to prevent falls and from getting caught in hanging window blind cords or draperies
- Hot water heater set so that water coming out of the faucet is no more than 120°F to reduce risk of scald burns
- Dressers and bookshelves secured to the wall with anti-tip devices

Always remember that even the best childproofing gadgets are no substitute for direct supervision of your twins. Do not be fooled into a false sense of security just because you have childproofed your home with all the right equipment—dangerous things can still happen. And certain household features are difficult to twinproof, requiring parents to be watchful and vigilant. For example, a simple bedroom door can cause problems. For a time, my twin boys enjoyed a gleeful but dangerous game in which they would each push on opposite sides of the same door. A foam guard didn't work at these locations, so we had to watch the boys vigilantly and guide them appropriately.

🐦 Returning to Work

The decisions of if and when to return to work after having a child are tricky enough, but even more complicated for parents of multiples. The cost of child care for 2 (or more!) kids can be significant, and many families who require 2 working parents need to explore all options and get creative with scheduling.

Options for child care include facility, home, or nanny or au pair. If you have 3 or more children, it may be most cost-effective to investigate the nanny or au pair options because your entire family will be covered, as opposed to paying additional rates for each added child. Visit sites, check references, interview with prepared questions, and follow your intuition when making your selection.

Once you've determined your child care and when you'll be returning to work, make sure to make a dry run of the new routine at least a week ahead of time and make necessary adjustments. When back in a working routine, ask your caregivers to take notes on your babies' daily schedules so you have a sense of practical matters such as their feeding and diaper change patterns as well as the fun stuff such as stroller rides and book preferences. Use special rituals to share special parent-child time when working parents return home from work. The nighttime bath or bedtime story is a perfect way for parents and babies to reconnect and bond after being apart during the daytime.

Toys and Books

Often, the best toys for babies are the toys that do the least. If the toy does less, your child does more. You do not need to spend a lot of money on toys even though you have 2 babies who are the same age. Babies love to explore simple things such as empty, clean yogurt containers and butter tubs. Place a block inside any empty container and shake it up—watch your babies' reactions! Simple containers teach your babies about spatial relationships and help them develop their fine motor skills as they reach for a rattle placed inside a bucket.

> ## Twin Tip!
> Infant twins' developmental stages help them share toys quite nicely! At the infant stages, your babies won't get jealous of each other's toys. You do not need to purchase 2 of each toy.

It is never too early to read to your babies. Have plenty of board books on hand, and leave the books around the home in each room so that you can pick one up and start reading at any given moment. Your twins can also find the books on their own and eventually turn pages and leaf through the pictures by themselves.

Twin Tip!

Get into the routine of visiting your local library frequently. You'll be pleasantly surprised by the board book selection for your infant twins. And best of all, the books are free! When you are feeling brave, you can bring your babies to an infant story time as well.

ﮔ Outings and Fun

Continue to make sure you get out of the house periodically to stay sane. Yes, there is still an outside world out there! Keep your diaper bag stocked so running off on a spontaneous errand is easier. You may love your twin stroller, but consider occasionally taking the twins out with a single stroller if you have one, with a front or backpack carrier. This way you can be a little more spry on your feet by not lugging around a huge double stroller. Also, the single stroller/carrier combo comes in handy if you're not in the mood for everyone staring at you and your family. It can't be helped—when

Twin Tip!

You're taking countless digital pictures of your twins. But who is who in each picture? Other parents of older twins would tell me, "Label your pictures quickly because down the line, you'll forget who is who!" But somehow in my sleep-deprived life with twin babies I couldn't get my act together to label the pictures. What I did do, though, was dress my identical twins in theme colors. Andrew mostly wore blue, and Ryan usually wore red. My pictures never did end up getting labels, but we always know that the little guy in blue is Andrew, and the cutie in red is Ryan. An added benefit—grandparents and friends picked up on our boys' color themes and when they visited us, they immediately knew who each boy was without an explanation!

people see twins they get so excited and will ask you lots of questions. Some days, the attention is fun, but other days, you just want to go about your business quickly. Personally, I have been told by countless strangers, "You sure have your hands full!" My standard response if I don't feel like talking? "We are very blessed," and I just keep moving along!

Continue Seeking Support

Do not be shy—ask family and friends for help. You are working very hard to care for your young twins, and you need breaks to stay fresh and healthy. If you do not have immediate family nearby available to help, you will need to think creatively for support. Investigate options through friends and neighbors in your community. Perhaps a family friend's preteen is interested in becoming a babysitter. She can get some hands-on training by being a mother's helper to your family. While you address other household chores, your mother's helper can read to your babies. An extra pair of hands can really help you during the infant stages, so do not be afraid to reach out for help.

Make sure you take time to connect with your spouse. A strong team works more effectively together. Communication is key, and relationships can be difficult when you're sleep deprived. Don't expect your spouse to read your mind—ask for specific help when you need it. Stewing over an ignored household chore is not allowed; simply talk about it in the open and ask for help in getting the chore completed.

Bonding With Each Twin

Keeping your twins on the same schedule when they are young infants has many wonderful benefits; however, always keep in the forefront of your mind that your twins are 2 unique individuals. Even at this early age, look for opportunities to connect with each of your twins as individuals. You can take one of your babies out alone for some special individual time while the other twin enjoys special one-on-one time with your spouse or another trusted adult caregiver. Special one-on-one time, even starting in infancy, can help you and each of your twins bond and get to know one another better.

Twin Tip!

Your twins are individuals. Even the language that you choose to refer to your twins can affect your (and others') impressions of them as individuals. Try not to refer to your children as "the twins"; rather, name them individually in conversation. Encourage family and friends to refer to your kids by name as well. If others ask you, "How are the twins?" you can respond, "Josh and Billy are great!"

When your twins are babies, you are synchronizing your twins' schedules for survival and sanity, but always remember to regard your twins as the 2 special people they are. As your babies approach the ages of 6 months old, you can start to ease out of survival mode somewhat and begin new family rituals of connecting with each of your twins on a one-on-one basis.

CHAPTER 5
Older Infancy
and First Birthday

Your miraculous twins' minds and bodies are growing at amazing rates from 6 months to their first birthday. New skills are learned at an incredible rate! Older babies seem to learn new things exponentially rather than merely sequentially. Whether your twins are identical or fraternal, they continue to evolve into 2 unique, individual people. Their distinct personalities are more evident each day.

For the first time in their young lives, your twins can truly illustrate their likes and dislikes to you. Sometimes, these illustrations might be quite crude, such as a swipe at a spoon full of food when they would rather not have another bite. Your twins will make you laugh each day. Your twins will keep you guessing each day as well! One twin will gobble down dinner with an extra helping, while the other eats a mere couple of bites and ends the meal.

The twins' smiles, coos, and early gestures form patterns of communication. This early communication creates true relationships with you, your family, and each other. As you nurture your twin babies' growth, you will see that as 2 unique individuals, each child will develop at his own rate.

❧ Sleep Patterns

Babies aged 6 months to the first birthday should be sleeping about 14 hours total in a 24-hour period to stay healthy and happy. About 11 of these hours should be spent in overnight sleep, and about 3 of these hours are divided up among daytime naps. The daytime sleep is usually divided into 2 naps, morning and afternoon. If you have older children, you may need to be flexible with the twins' nap schedule because of the older kids' carpooling and school activities, but do your best to be as respectful to your twins' sleep requirements as you can. If your twins get their necessary sleep, everyone will be happier.

Just as in early infancy, your twin babies' usual sleep routines may be temporarily disrupted in times of illness or travel. Once the twins are over their illness or you are back home from a trip, get everyone back on board with your usual sleep routine. Sometimes babies can get accustomed to parents tending to them in the middle of the night if they have been congested, coughing, or feverish. When they are healthy once again, help your twin babies get themselves back to sleep. If you need a refresher on good sleep hygiene habits for your twins, please refer to the previous chapter.

The strategies to encourage good sleep habits are helpful if implemented anytime during infancy, not just the early months. Older babies now understand object permanence, and they know that their parents exist even when they are not in the room with them. Your twins may holler for you to pick them up in the middle of the night, or they might even resist bedtime, but make sure you keep your bedtime and nighttime rituals consistent. Evening baths, pajamas, story time, and perhaps a song or two, followed by sweet goodnight kisses are all that your twins need to tuck them in for the night.

Twin Tip!

Your older twin babies are babbling and communicating more. You may notice at bedtime, after you say goodnight and close the door, your twins are babbling, talking, to one another. These exchanges between your twins are adorable and are just one example of the special joys parents of twins get to experience! Listen at the door if you like, but don't feel the need to reenter the room and shush your babies. They are experimenting with their early language skills. They may chitchat together for a good 30 minutes, but as long as they fall asleep eventually, you don't need to interrupt them.

ஃ Mealtime: A Whole New World

Your twin babies' nutrition from 6 months up to their first birthday should consist of continued breast milk or infant formula, as well as an increasing variety and amount of solid foods. In addition, table foods should slowly be introduced. It is hard to believe, but by the time your twins turn 1 year old, they should be eating mostly table foods. If growth and development have been normal, your twins should continue drinking breast milk or infant formula up to the first birthday. Breast milk and infant formula have all the specialized nutrients in just the right proportions, something especially important if your twins were born small or premature. After the first birthday, your twins should be able to switch to vitamin D whole milk.

You will notice that your twins' feeding patterns may begin to change over this period of late infancy. They may noticeably nurse less or drink less formula in a 24-hour period. This is normal and happens for 3 reasons.

- Your twins are eating more solid foods and are more interested in table foods. They are beginning to form taste preferences and may prefer the excitement of a new table food to the same old routine milk they always drink. Your twins are also mastering the art of self-feeding. The focus should be placed on their increasing independence, not their total caloric intake.

- Your twins are more active and interested in the world around them. They are working on developing their fine motor skills, perfecting their pincer grasp, and examining microscopic pieces of fuzz. They would rather crawl around and pull themselves up on the coffee table to see the toy sitting on top. Exploration can be a lot more fun than eating or drinking!

- All babies start to slow their rate of growth as they approach their first birthday. Because the child is not growing quite so quickly, she simply won't have the desire to eat as much as she did a couple of months earlier.

We as parents tend to worry about our kids' eating habits and wonder why a kid who ate a certain amount in the past is now eating less. At this age, you need to know that drinking less milk is to be expected.

Parents of twins must also always remind themselves not to compare the 2 children. Do not be surprised or overly concerned if one twin drinks more or less milk than the other. Remember that you have 2 different babies who happen to be the same age, but everyone is an individual! If you have persistent worries, check with your pediatrician.

Monitor your twins' total intake of formula in a 24-hour period. After the first birthday, when the switch is made to whole cow's milk,

> ## *Twin Tip!*
> Expect your twins to have different appetites on differ-
> ent days. Your twins will also weigh different amounts.
> As long as growth has been healthy, don't fret about the
> "skinnier" twin!

you will be looking for a target maximum of 16 to 18 ounces of milk a day (definitely not more than 24 ounces in a day, which increases the risk of iron deficiency anemia). Plan ahead and make sure that the twins' liquid diet is being tapered if it is approaching those numbers before the first birthday.

How will you transition your twins' milk after their first birthday? Some parents switch to cow's milk cold turkey after the first birthday. However, some babies do not transition to a new-tasting milk so easily. For our family, I have used a system of mixing formula with whole milk, over time increasing the proportion of whole milk to formula. I found that my kids were more willing to accept the new taste if it was introduced more gradually. Over a couple of weeks' time, change the composition of your 6-ounce bottles, for example, from 5 ounces of formula plus 1 ounce milk to 4 ounces of formula plus 2 ounces milk, and so on until the proportion of the bottle becomes 100% whole milk. This method works with a minimum of resistance from your twins because the taste change has been made over time.

ᴈ◗ Solid and Table Foods

From 6 months and up, your twins should be eating new foods each week. Introduce a single new food every 3 to 5 days to ensure that there is no food allergy or intolerance. Traditionally pediatricians had recommended a specific order for new foods to be introduced— starting with infant cereals mixed with breast milk or formula, then moving on to pureed and strained vegetables, followed by pureed and strained fruits, followed by meats, then lastly table foods. More recently, however, experts are agreeing that a specific order of introduction is not required. No required order of food type is good news for busy parents of twins—one less rule that you need to stress out about! Relax, do not worry about introducing foods in a specific order, and just ensure that you are serving your twins a good variety of food groups and flavors. You are enhancing your babies' palates as well as providing good nutrition.

While the specific order of foods may not be important to your twins, a good source of iron is. Infant cereals are a great source of iron. At 6 months your twins need a new, additional source of iron to accommodate their growth and red blood cell production, which is especially important for breastfed babies. Mix infant cereals such as rice and oatmeal with pumped breast milk or infant formula instead of plain water to boost the caloric and nutritional value. In addition, your twins are accustomed to the flavor of the milk or formula and will happily recognize the familiar flavor in the new taste of cereal.

Twin Tip!

If the weather is nice, feed your twins outside as much as you can! Two babies eating solid foods can get quite messy, and life is easier if you don't have to mop up the floor perfectly after each meal. For indoor meals, some parents like to put a shower curtain or other similar tarp on the floor underneath the 2 high chairs to streamline post-meal cleanup.

In addition to a good source of iron, your twins need fluoride supplementation starting at 6 months of age. If your home water supply is treated municipal water, your fluoride needs are most likely met. If you use well water, you should ask your pediatrician if your twins need a fluoride-multivitamin supplement. More fluoride is not necessarily better, however—babies can develop fluorosis, a condition harmful to teeth and bones, if they receive too much fluoride. Speak with your pediatrician to make sure you have the right balance of fluoride.

Your twins should be ready to try table finger foods around the age of 9 months. To start eating finger foods, they should be able to sit up fully and have a good pincer grasp. O-shaped breakfast cereal is a good first finger food because it quickly melts in the mouth, minimizing the risk of choking. To prevent choking, always cut up table foods into lengthwise, manageable sizes for your twins, and make sure foods are cooked well and on the mushy side. You may personally prefer your vegetables with a nice crunch, but for now, serve your twin babies mushy vegetables!

Do not be surprised if your twins have different taste preferences! Your twins are unique individuals after all. Offer an interesting variety of tastes, textures, and flavors at mealtimes. If one or both of your twins reject a food the first time it is offered, do not write off that food just yet. They may not be crazy about green beans the first couple of times they taste it, but keep trying on different occasions. Experts agree that it can take a dozen tries of a new food before a child decides that he likes it. And even from the time that your twins are babies, avoid power struggles at mealtimes.

> ## *Twin Tip!*
> Your twin babies love to mimic you. One day soon they will try to feed each other!

When your twins are seated in their high chairs eating, never leave the room, even for a moment. You never know when one twin may choke on a bit of food. Sometimes, having 2 babies in the house, we can have a false sense of security, as if there is safety in numbers. Always make sure that an adult directly supervises your twins' mealtimes.

☙ Sippy Cup Training — Bye-bye, Bottles!

Your twins are ready to learn how to drink from a sippy cup around their first birthday. Why do pediatricians encourage families to move forward from the bottle at this age? As babies grow older and become more attached to certain people and certain objects, they tend to form stronger bonds with these objects. Unfortunately a young child may rely on the bottle for *comfort* in addition to nutrition, and pediatricians have seen that prolonged exposure to the bottle can cause problems such as excessive weight gain and dental cavities. If a child is sucking on a bottle habitually, the milk or juice inside can cause decay of new teeth, which is known as early childhood caries.

As they approach the first birthday, your children need to learn a more mature way of drinking milk. Milk should be enjoyed at standard mealtimes and snack times while sitting upright at a high chair or table. A child should drink and eat at the high chair or table until he feels full, and then he can leave the table to go do other things. A child cannot learn effectively or master new skills if he always has one hand holding a bottle.

A transition to a sippy cup is easier if done sooner rather than later, and as a parent of twins, you can make your life easier by making the transition sooner. The later you make the transition from a bottle to a cup, the more difficult it will be because 1-year-olds develop their sense of authority more strongly each month. Changing bottles to sippy cups around the time of your twins' first birthday should help to make the process more relaxed for all of you.

When you initiate your twins' sippy cup training sessions, you need to start small and work your way up. Initially, select a bottle-feeding session that is not a major feeding—maybe a mid-afternoon feeding. You do not want your twins to be so hungry that they get

Twin Tip!

As a parent of twins you are always on a quest for efficiency. The transition to sippy cups may initially seem like a lot of hassle or effort, and you may be tempted to keep handing your twins bottles to drink, especially if they have figured out how to hold the bottles themselves. Remember that the sooner they learn how to drink from sippy cups, the further they are down the road to independence. When your twins are more independent, you can use your time to play and interact with them, rather than to continue routine tasks of feeding and cleaning. Which option is more fun?

frustrated at the cup-learning process. Many sippy cup brands have a separate valve insert that is placed inside the lid to prevent spills. Make training easier for your kids and don't use the valve insert at first. These valves prevent milk from flowing freely from the spout and require that the child use more sucking action to pull the milk out. Not using the valve can be a bit messier, but you want to help your twins understand that this new object's purpose is to give them milk and relieve their thirst, even before they can master the proper sucking action.

What about logistics? Seat your twins in their high chairs in front of you and alternate attempting to drink from the cup or playing with each child. The training sessions should be a pleasant and fun experience because you always want your children to have positive associations with mealtimes. If you find that the twins are getting frustrated or swiping at the cup, or that you yourself are getting annoyed, end the session. You can try again tomorrow. Or if one twin would rather crawl around while the other is interested and actually taking some sips of milk, go ahead and use this opportunity with the interested twin. One-on-one time with each child is always a good thing!

There are a few methods for ultimately making the switch from nursing or bottle-feeding to cup drinking, and every family must choose the method that will work for them, logistically and emotionally. As with most parenting issues, no one solution can fit everybody well, and one size doesn't fit all.

Some advise a cold turkey approach, claiming that if the breast or a bottle is continued to be offered at any time of day in any way, it will cause the child to yearn for it and hold out for it, preventing the child from getting used to the new method of drinking. I feel that this cold turkey method is a bit harsh on parents and children. In the case of nursing, it will also cause the mother a great deal of physical pain because a mom will likely suffer from some breast engorgement and leaking if nursing is terminated abruptly from 4 sessions a day to none.

A kinder and gentler approach to wean your twins is to gradually switch the style of drinking one session at a time until eventually all the feeding sessions have been replaced with a cup. As mentioned

> ## *Twin Tip!*
>
> Your twins have many transitions to make during their early years. Whether it is learning to drink from a sippy cup, toilet training, or moving to a big-kid bed, you as a parent need to be aware of your emotions. Transitioning 2 kids through the same thing at the same time is tough! If you find yourself getting frustrated or annoyed, you need to take a step back and regroup. Even young babies can pick up on parental anxiety, and the transition will be that much tougher to make. Do your best to calm down, take a break, and try again another day.

earlier, start with a feeding that usually is lighter so that hunger doesn't upset your twins into being unwilling to try something new. Try this new drinking method at the same session each day for a week or so, and then select a different time of day to switch drinking styles. You can lengthen or shorten the time between additional sessions as you need to make it work for your family. If relatives are visiting for a weekend or some other event is going on, it is fine to wait an additional week here or there as needed to let everyone adjust to the new system. You won't want to switch a morning bottle-feeding to a cup feeding at a time when a lot of other things are happening, say at Thanksgiving. If you make things a bit easier on yourself, you will be a happier parent to help your twins get through the transition. Over time, the switch will eventually be made for all the feeding sessions of the day.

If you are still nursing, you will notice that once you drop a session or two, your milk supply may take a precipitous dip. You may find that you will need to offer sippy cups more quickly than you had planned. Try not to fret about the total volume of milk that the twins drink. Remember that their growth rates are slowing down, and if they are truly hungry, they'll figure out a way to drink! Your twins are also eating solid foods, so they won't starve. Many nursing moms hold onto one last nursing session, usually at bedtime, for emotional bonding and comfort—a great ritual if you wish to continue it.

ॐ Oral Health

Your twins' first teeth may come in, on average, around the time they are 6 months old. Every child is different, so do not be concerned if your twins get their first teeth a little sooner or later. Ask your pediatrician about any concerns you might have. You can start using an infant toothbrush with fluoride-free toothpaste twice a day when the first tooth has come in. Even better than a toothbrush at this young age is simply gently rubbing the teeth and gums with an infant washcloth and water. Get in the habit of cleaning your twins' gums and early teeth with a clean washcloth after a meal. Your babies are probably quite messy with sticky cereal and pureed fruits all over their faces after a meal, and you are wiping them down anyway. Use a fresh washcloth and clean the gums and teeth. We dedicated an entire kitchen drawer to fresh, clean infant washcloths to simplify post-meal cleanups.

> ## *Twin Tip!*
> As a parent of twin babies, you perform many of the same child care tasks each day. Step back and evaluate where you store necessary baby supplies. Could you reorganize frequently used items to make them more accessible and streamline caring for your twins?

ॐ Play and Development

When your twins start to sit independently, usually around the 6-month mark, they will be able to view the world from an entirely new vantage point! I can promise you that your twins will achieve this milestone on different days—do not fret or compare the two. My son Andrew sat up alone a full month or so before his twin brother Ryan. I will admit I was a nervous wreck wondering when little Ryan would sit up by himself! Now that we are looking back, I laugh when I remember how worried I was about Ryan's motor development— today he is as strong and capable as any kid on a playground!

A cause of concern for many parents of singletons and multiples is wondering when their children will take their first steps. Much

Twin Tip!

When your twins are both sitting up independently, you can do cool new things that will make your life easier. For example, you can fill your big bathtub and bathe them at the same time. Never get a false sense of security, though—continue to always attend to your children when they are in or near the bathtub and stay within arm's reach. Soon you will also be able to introduce activity centers (seats surrounded by 360 degrees of toys!). Bathing both babies simultaneously or having a new fun place for your babies to spend time while you make dinner are the sorts of things that will streamline your life and make the daily routine easier.

importance has been placed on the walking motor milestone throughout generations. You'll often hear grandparents chuckle, "Oh, he didn't walk until 15 months," or others proudly brag, "My daughter walked at 10 months," as if walking makes her a genius. Walking has no relation to intelligence or future motor dexterity! Walking can start anywhere from 9 to 18 months and still be considered normal. Each child develops at his own rate!

Many parents' anxieties over this issue are fueled at family get-togethers where they hear about similar-aged cousins' physical feats, or at playdates with friends, because the urge to compare your child with others is irresistible. What is more, parents of twins have 2 cute little specimens under their noses, and it is human nature to compare them to each other. Try not to do it. Even if your twins are identical, they both need their own time to get where they need to go. The twin who walks first is not better or smarter. The one who walks later will not need special assistance throughout her life.

On average, twins may start walking a bit later than their similarly aged single-born peers. I believe this is for 2 reasons. First, many twins are born early or preterm, putting their development on a slightly different schedule. Second, when you have 2 babies to keep an eye on, it is simply more difficult to give them individual training

> ## *Twin Tip!*
>
> When it comes to milestones, you will notice that over time, you will frequently find yourself comparing the twins with each other. And the comparisons won't end any time soon. Who will count to 100 first? Who will learn to read first? Assuming your twins are generally healthy, they will probably alternate who masters a new skill first. Trust me when I tell you that in the long run, you will be amazed at the fact that each child will take the lead in different areas, and alternate being the leader, so to speak; *it will all balance out.* One may learn to ride a tricycle independently earlier, for example, while the other shows a knack for drawing shapes and pictures first. Enjoy your child's achievement for what it is, without fretting over why her twin hasn't done it yet. Parents of different-aged children experience these comparisons among their children as well, but not with the intensity with which we parents of twins can compare our children.

sessions. Parents of just one baby have the luxury of being able to hold both of their child's hands and coach him to walk all day long, encouraging a new desire to walk with support. Parents of multiples are not able to focus such attention on one child.

Look at it this way—parents of more than one kid, born at different ages, don't even have such time to devote to one single baby. My fourth child is a singleton. Did I ever have time to hold her hands for more than 5 minutes to help her learn to walk around the house? Definitely not! And she figured it out anyway. Don't worry, it will happen. But do ask your pediatrician about any special concerns you may have about your twins' motor development.

Exersaucers are toys that our family enjoyed when our twin boys were older infants. These stationary toy centers have a baby seat in the center and are surrounded by colorful toys, music boxes, and activities. These can be pricey and it may be too expensive to buy 2. We used our old one from our oldest son and borrowed one from my sister-in-law's family. Your twins can bounce safely in these toy

> ## Twin Tip!
>
> One day you will laugh at yourself that you were ever pining for your twins to walk! Soon enough, they will be 2 years old and running top speed in opposite directions!

centers, whacking the buttons on the music boxes and having fun together, and you'll know where they are—no wondering if they've crawled into the bathroom and stuck their hand in the toilet. Make sure your twins don't spend more than 15 minutes at a stretch in these toy centers, though—your twins do need to move about the house developing their muscles and coordination. But for hectic times such as fixing the family dinner, it was a real helper for me to have my twin boys happily and safely playing for 15 minutes. We have hilarious home videos of our twins bouncing in tandem while giggling madly.

Do not confuse these stationary play centers with old-fashioned walkers that can wheel about the house. Walkers are extremely dangerous, and many children have broken bones or suffered serious head injuries from falling down stairs in walkers. Contrary to the old thinking, walkers do not assist a child in walking earlier. In fact, the walker uses different muscle groups than those used in natural walking and will delay independent walking.

> ## Twin Tip!
>
> The American Academy of Pediatrics has recommended banning the sale of infant walkers. Do not buy one, and do not let any family members hand one down to you.

☙ Language and Communication

When it comes to twins' language development, parents may hear concerning generalizations that twins sometimes have language delays compared with their singleton peers, boys more so than girls. Take these generalizations for what they are and focus on *your* unique children and their abilities.

How can you encourage your twins' early language skills? Narrate experiences to your twins, providing a running dialogue of the day's events, no matter how mundane they may be. "Now we're changing your diaper." "That little dog is barking."

Well before your children utter their first words, they have a growing *receptive* vocabulary of words, meaning that they understand what you are saying even if they are not yet talking themselves! You may be mentioning a particular toy to your spouse, and your child may surprise you by crawling over to that toy. You will notice that your twins are starting to imitate words and babble with conversational inflections, as if they are truly saying something. Encourage these early discussions, as they will evolve over time to become the real deal!

Some twins may have an early language delay because of a lack of manpower—twins simply outnumber a parent 2 to 1, making it logistically difficult to get as much meaningful one-on-one time for talking as a single-born baby would get. The chaos in the daily household routine can make encouraging language development a real challenge. Most days, you're not so concerned with the kids' language skills as you are with trying to make it to bedtime with the house intact!

Twin Tip!

How do you handle teaching your twins how to talk while life is so crazy? Narrate the events of your daily lives. Your house is hectic—*talk* about it with your twins! "Boy, this room is messy." "Can you believe I haven't showered in 2 days?"

Get as much one-on-one time as possible with each of your twins. Unless you have 4 hands, you change only one twin's diaper at one time—diaper changes can be a special opportunity to really look into her eyes and talk to her while you change her. Her twin will get his chance when he gets his diaper changed. It's all about capturing teachable moments.

Studies have shown that some twins may have an early language delay, but most of these kids do catch up by 4 or 5 years of age. If you have particular concerns about your twins' language development, talk to your pediatrician to determine if further evaluation or therapy will be needed.

᎒ Safety Issues

As your twins are becoming more mobile each day, it becomes more critical to make sure they are constantly supervised. Always monitor your home to make sure the childproofing is as good as it can be, and make adjustments as needed. There will always be areas that require protection or modification that you didn't think of, but one of your twins will helpfully demonstrate to you! It may be a bummer to put away your wine rack for now, but good childproofing will make your life easier in the long run. A well-childproofed home allows your twins more freedom to explore and allows parents to avoid redirecting their children all day long.

Twin Tip!

Remember that the best childproofing in the world does not replace direct supervision. Paper clips or other small choking hazards can accidentally fall on the ground, ready for inspection by your 10-month-olds. Your twins are little scientist-explorers, making discoveries and charting new territories, but they have little to no sense of what is safe and what is not.

Don't forget that there is childproofing and there is twinproofing. Every month your twins are getting smarter, and they will learn as much from their twin's experiences as from their own! They will each try out more things around the house than a singleton because they like to try what their twin just did. Also keep in mind that a pressure-mounted gate that keeps a singleton baby out of a formal room full of breakable knickknacks may not continue to hold against the combined weight of 2 little ones leaning and pushing on it!

> ## *Twin Tip!*
> Creatively assess your home to see if you can create a safe designated play area for your growing twins. Safety gates come in a wide assortment and allow parents to contain kids in a particular zone. We did not have a formal living room set up in our home while our kids were young, so it was logical for us to use the space instead as a play area.

Now that your twins are becoming increasingly mobile as they crawl with greater speed and are learning to walk, it is nice to maintain some sort of safe zone in which to plop your twins when you cannot keep an eagle eye on them. If you have to run to the bathroom or retrieve something from the hot oven, one of your twins will find a loose button on the carpet at that exact moment and pop it in his mouth for further exploration. To prevent such an ill-timed disaster, keep a large gated play yard area set up in some corner of your home.

> ## *Twin Tip!*
> Singleton parents can get away with using a portable playpen as a temporary safe zone, but alas, parents of multiples need more real estate than a small rectangle!

Several options of gated play yards are commercially available; another option is to gate off a closely inspected safe corner of a room. Your twins may not spend a lot of time playing in the safe zone, but it is good to have the space prepared and ready when you do need it. Keep special baby-safe toys inside, and even rotate toys into the space as needed to keep your twins interested. Inspect the play area multiple times a day for surprise choking hazards that may have appeared, such as from a broken toy or an older sibling who brought his Lego bricks nearby.

🕊 Discipline—Working Toward Acceptable Behaviors

At this age, your twins do not need discipline in the traditional sense, but you do need to start teaching your twins what is and is not appropriate. It is more difficult to undo bad habits if they have been tolerated even a small number of times in the past. I have used the concept of house rules for our family. Everyone in the house must follow the house rules to stay safe. Instead of saying "no" repeatedly (which is a great way to teach the word quickly, by the way—you will be hearing it said back to you often if you're not judicious with the use of the word), I try to phrase my instructions differently. "We don't touch the oven door—it's hot." "Don't pull my hair—it hurts mommy's head."

Twin Tip!

Babies' early infractions are usually just the result of early explorers acting on their natural and healthy curiosity— but parents of twins need to draw the line of what is and is not OK. The oven door window is shiny, reflective, and very interesting to an 11-month-old, but even if it is currently off, you don't want your twins thinking it is OK to lean on it and look at it up close. One of these days it *will* be hot, and you may not be right there to intervene.

When your twins engage in inappropriate behavior, intervene *immediately* so that your children connect the action with the consequence. Remove your child from the situation, and redirect your child to a new activity or location. Redirection works well because kids this age still have a short attention span.

Sometimes parents are caught off guard by a pull to the hair or a bite to the shoulder by a child, and in the confusion of the moment may have even laughed. Be careful to avoid this if you can! Your child will think what she has done is funny or somehow good. The child will replicate the action to see if she can get you to laugh again.

Biting is not a great habit to encourage! Avert your face if you cannot suppress a laugh, and try to be as consistent in your responses as you can. In the case of biting, remove the child from your shoulder and firmly say, "No. We do not bite." At times, the word "no" is appropriate, if used selectively and sporadically.

Consistency is especially important when you have 2 kids the same age learning the house rules. Two little ones running about can quickly escalate to mayhem without parents actively supervising, intervening, and redirecting. Lessons learned at a young age will carry into the next few years and make your life easier over the long haul.

Twin Tip!

It is easier to encourage good behavior now than to have to undo bad behavior down the line.

Do not unwittingly encourage behavior that you do not want repeated endlessly in the future. If you laugh and say how cute it is when your twins pull on your vertical blinds at 10 months, be prepared for two 22-month-old toddlers to be yanking on them regularly in the future, unless some sort of house rule has been established early on.

Twin Tip!

As simple as it sounds, consistency in your response is key. It sounds simple, but it really is not that simple. It is much harder to be consistent when you are fatigued and overworked, running after your twins all day. There will be days when you will be tired and not feeling like being on the ball, but these are the days that you have still got to be on your A game and continue to enforce consistent rules.

✑ Your Emotions — How to Stay Sane

The constant supervision of more than one crawling, mobile baby can take a toll on parents. When your multiples start crawling and walking, you will need the constant surveillance and vigilance of an air traffic controller—and note that air traffic controller is regarded as one of the most stressful occupations! As with any job or task, to stay fresh, it is important to take breaks. Our theme of *asking for help* comes into play again. Do not consider it a sign of being anything less than a great parent; consider it extremely wise to be able to identify those particularly stressful times when the whole family would benefit from one or both parents getting a break.

Ask your spouse for help. Spouses can and should be able to handle the house and all the kids for any stretch of time. Your children's father, for example, is not babysitting because he is a parent! Do you have relatives or trusted good friends who live nearby? Is there a friendly neighborhood tween looking for mother's helper experience before full-fledged babysitting? Investigate all your options for assistance.

What constitutes a break? That is up to you. You could spend an hour with a good book, take a neighborhood run, go to the coffee shop for a couple of hours, spend an evening out with friends, or take an overnight trip (see, I have plenty of ideas!).

> # *Twin Tip!*
> Take little and big breaks as needed—doctor's orders! As we say in our house, "If Mommy's not happy, *nobody's* happy!"

Asking for help and taking parenting breaks is healthy for you to step back and take a look at how your family is affecting your emotions. Personally, I have experienced a special kind of guilt starting from the time that my twins were born. When I am able to spend some time one-on-one with one boy snuggling, reading a book together, or showing him how I mix the pancake batter, there are times I cannot truly enjoy the moment because I already feel guilty that I am not spending this special time with the other guy as well. Sometimes I'll find myself interrupting the special moment to invite the other twin to join us, or I hurry through the moment so I can grab the twin and replicate the moment for him. Of course, interruptions and rushing do not result in meaningful, spontaneous bonding and teaching moments. It just results in one or both twins running off elsewhere while I am left sitting there with the book asking, "Doesn't anyone want to read with Mommy?" What have I learned from this? If you've got one of your twins on your lap ready for a story, *go ahead and start reading*. Over time, there will be plenty of opportunities for the other twin to get his own lap time as well.

> ## *Twin Tip!*
>
> Focus on the *collection of experiences* each twin has over time—the balance will not necessarily be perfectly equal, but it should be fair. And each of your twins deserves as much alone time with you as possible. Get over the guilt and enjoy the special time—one-on-one time provides major teachable moments and encourages relationships within your family.

Especially if you are a stay-at-home parent, I'm sure that you have never felt as housebound as you have this year. If you were on bed rest during your pregnancy, that can just add to your feelings of being disconnected from the outside world. On a certain level, it may seem easier to never leave the house again! Why would you leave? The milk is in the fridge, the stack of diapers is at the ever-ready changing table, and extra clothes are in the drawers. Packing up your twins for any sort of outing can just seem like a lot of hassle. But even if it is just a few times a month, do make the effort to take your babies out of the house. It may be as mundane as walking around the mall for 20 minutes, but these experiences will be healthy for you and your twins.

If you are feeling really adventurous, enlist your spouse or other adult to help the family go to a local pool. It may be daunting to plan, prepare, and execute the outing—frankly, it will feel like you are planning a small military operation—but it will be mentally energizing for all involved.

Twin Tip!

When our twins were babies, it was always surprising to my husband and me how calm and focused our twins seemed to be after even just a simple trip to a sandwich shop. Just like for adults, taking twin 11-month-olds out of their usual environment and routine can help them refresh and refocus. They can then come back to their familiar play areas and toys with a new perspective and a new appreciation.

⁂ Special Time With Each Twin

A child who receives plenty of positive one-on-one time will be less likely to act out in other areas to receive negative attention. Attention, whether positive or negative, is what your twins crave from you. These one-on-one moments of positive interaction are also needed so you can start to recognize the individual and unique traits that each twin has. Even identical twins can have very different ways of looking at the world.

How can a busy family squeeze in one-on-one time with each child? Get creative and look for new ways each week. Every family needs to grocery shop periodically. You can rotate turns each week for special one-on-one shopping trips with a parent. One child gets a fun outing, seeing all the excitement at the store and learning colors and numbers as you select 4 green apples to put in a bag, while the other child gets playtime with the caregiver at home. You won't need to feel guilty about it because the next weekend, it will be the other twin's turn to go. If a relative lives nearby, perhaps he can stay home with one twin while you take the other for a walk to talk about things you see in the neighborhood, squeezing in a bit of healthy exercise as well.

೭☙ The First Birthday

Congratulations! You have survived the first year with twins! Relish their first birthday as a time to pat yourself on the back. Take a look at your home videos and laugh at how large your pregnant belly was! Smile at your 2 beautiful children who just happened to be born on the same day, and look how far you have all come!

If you are going to have a party, make it a small party in the middle of the day. You won't be overwhelmed, the twins won't be overwhelmed, and you can all enjoy the day. Do your children a favor and make sure you bake or purchase 2 birthday cakes, one for each of them. Be sure to take photos of each twin alone with her cake, as well as together with both cakes. In our family, we even alternate who gets sung to first each year.

Twin Tip!

When the twins are grown, they will appreciate that you treated them as individuals and not as a unit by singing "Happy Birthday" for each of them specifically. Singing twice also sends a message to your family and friends at the party who may have a tendency to refer to your completely individual children as "the twins."

೭☙ Year One—An Extraordinary Time That Flies By!

It is a cliché because it is *true*—these early days of your babies' lives go by very fast! I believe that the time flies even faster than it does with a single-born baby because you are just so busy. Of course you will have days where you think your twins will never sit unsupported, never hold onto a sippy cup and drink by themselves, never talk! But then you will turn around one day and everything has suddenly changed—they are now running after each other pretending to be puppies, barking loudly, laughing hysterically.

You will want to keep 2 simple baby books to jot down funny notes and stories. I was too busy to keep perfect baby books, but I

> # *Twin Tip!*
> If everything is going wrong, the house is a mess, and your babies are wearing pajamas all day every day, just laugh and enjoy it! Think of all the great stories you will have for family lore. Your children will never remember how clean your house was growing up—they will remember how much fun they had with you.

did have a system to make frequent updates to each twin's separate book. If one of my twins did something cute, I would jot it down on a note pad. I would pile up my notes and once every couple of months I would take the collection of notes and write the items all at once in the baby books.

Invariably when you take your twins out into the world, people will be interested in your crazy little family. The best encounters for me are from parents who have had twins themselves who are now grown. I remember when an older gentleman spied my husband and me eating lunch in a casual restaurant with our 2-year-old and 12-month-old twins. He approached us when he and his wife were leaving and told us that they had twins with a closely spaced older brother, and they were all grown up now. He paused, gave a sly grin, and said, "It's a lot of fun, isn't it?"

It really helps to know that other people have not only survived your situation, but also enjoyed it and lived to tell about it. It is easy to feel isolated, especially if you are staying home with your twins. The feelings of isolation are normal and will soon be replaced by the hustle and bustle of your twins' toddler and preschool years to come.

&❧ CHAPTER 6

The Toddler Years
(1- and 2-Year-Olds)

With each passing month and each passing year, life with your twins gets easier and easier. The daytime routine has an increasingly consistent rhythm and flow. Using a fairly dependable schedule, children and parents alike can predict what will happen next. Everyone will get along more harmoniously with a good home schedule because everyone is on the same page. At nighttime, your toddler twins are old enough to sleep through the night consistently and regularly. The more sleep everyone gets at night, mom and dad included, the happier everyone will be!

That being said, life with twins does not become easier in a straightforward manner. On the whole, the day-to-day routine gets easier, but the transitions of the toddler years provide some bumps in the road—discipline and toilet training, for example. Is it easier to care for 15-month-old twins than 3-month-old twins? Yes, but 15-month-olds have their own set of issues with which to contend.

One- and 2-year-old children have an increasing sense of self—each child is realizing that she is a person separate from her parents and her twin. As your children have a growing sense of the fact that they are independent individuals, they seek to separate themselves from their parents and twin. This independence may sometimes exhibit itself in unpleasant ways.

The toddler years can be exciting and scary for your twins. Your role as a parent is to continue to provide the same loving, secure environment as you did in their infancy, while showing them what is appropriate behavior. Your patience, coupled with gentle encouragement, will help guide your toddler twins to mature and grow into well-behaved preschoolers. There will be some challenges during your twins' toddler years, but try not to get too frustrated on the difficult days. Enjoy your children and watch with amazement how quickly they are learning new things!

❧ Sleep Issues

A child who sleeps well is healthier, gets along with others more easily, and is ready to play and learn. Your twins' nap time is sacred. A regular, consistent sleep schedule keeps your children happy and

Twin Tip!

Keep in mind that every family schedule has different needs. When your twins are toddlers, you may need to shift from 2 naps a day to 1 major early afternoon nap a day because of a resistance to the morning nap or to accommodate an older child's schedule needs. Look at your family's schedule to determine the best way to provide your twins with 14 hours of sleep each 24-hour day. Parents who work outside the home may choose to give their kids an early afternoon nap until they are 5 years old, so that they can have some quality family time in the evenings without the kids being overtired.

healthy, and can save parents' sanity. No matter how crazy your days are, there is a predictable chunk of time each day that you know you can work on your to-do list, put away laundry, or take a nap yourself!

As your twins grow into toddlers with new interests and abilities, life is getting more exciting and the idea of sleep becomes less appealing. Your formerly agreeable nappers may suddenly resist the idea of some midday slumber. Do not mistake this disinterest as a sign that they don't need naps anymore. One- and 2-year-olds still require an average of 14 hours of sleep every day, in the form of 11 to 12 hours of overnight sleep, and 1 or 2 naps a day totaling 2 to 3 hours in length. Every child is different, but some kids may give up naps around 2½ or 3 years of age.

If your twins are resisting nap time or bedtime, remember that overtired kids may actually have more difficulty falling asleep than well-rested children. If your toddler twins are more resistant at nap time, you may want to consider starting nap time earlier to see if they'll go down more easily. Give yourself room to experiment to find out the best solution for your family. If your twins are particularly cranky one week, poor sleep may be the culprit. Try a few days with earlier nap times and bedtimes and see what happens. If your twins are pretty happy with the new schedule, you can be more confident that they're getting enough rest.

If your toddler twins are sleeping well in their cribs, and are not yet climbing out, leave them in their cribs! Some parents celebrate the second birthday with big-kid beds, but I speak from experience when I tell you that big-kid beds will introduce a whole new set of sleep issues! I recommend letting your twins enjoy their cribs as long as possible (as long as the twins are remaining safely in their cribs), but do be prepared for the big-kid bed transition. You never know when the day that they learn to climb out of their cribs will arrive! When one twin learns how to hop out of the crib, her twin will learn right alongside by watching her. If you don't have big-kid beds ready yet and your twins start climbing out of their cribs, a safe, temporary transition is to simply remove the cribs from the room and place the crib mattresses directly on the floor. This will reduce the risk of injuries from falls.

Twin Tip!

It is in everyone's best interests—your twins, mom and dad, and siblings—that a reliable sleep schedule continue as the twins grow older. The benefits extend beyond the twins and parents. For our family, when our twins were 1-year-olds, their nap time was ideal for one-on-one time with our oldest son, who was 3 years old at the time. Toddler twins have a way of occupying their parents' complete attention while they are awake; their nap time is a perfect time to give their sibling(s) some much-needed attention. Nap time is also a nice chunk of time to play those board games that toddlers tend to destroy, or at a minimum, mess up the cards and move the players' pieces. Your twins' nap time can be the time to bring out the toys with small parts (to a designated area) that are too difficult to have around when the toddlers of the house are awake. Everyone will become quite adept at cleaning up the choking hazards before the twins wake up from their naps.

⮞ Transitioning to Big-Kid Beds

Transitioning our twin boys from cribs into big-kid beds was a very challenging time for our family. Even when my twin boys were still infants, I looked ahead and had a great deal of respect for, and fear of, this momentous milestone, having lived through our oldest son's transition. I recalled many a night of our little guy at our bedside at 3:00 am simply because he had the freedom to do so! I was dreading the twins' realization of "I'm free! *We're* free! No crib rails! All-night party!" Or, on the flip side, the twins could be afraid of their new environment—switching to an open bed with no secure, tall rails to keep one safe can be scary for a 2-year-old. So whether your twins are elated or terrified that it's 2:00 am and they've found themselves awake in a new bed, chances are they'll do one of these things: have

Twin Tip!

Some families successfully try gimmicks to keep their twins in their new big-kid beds. A family we know with triplets (including 2 boys who shared a bedroom) recommended that we get car beds for our twin boys—plastic molded twin-size beds in the shape of a car. Apparently, their boys were so in love with their car beds that it never occurred to them to climb out of bed in the middle of the night. These car beds sounded so magical that we budgeted the steep price of 2 car beds, thinking that money toward a good night's sleep would be money well spent. To make a long story short, these car beds did not prove to be so magical for my family. We experienced nighttime parties (with draperies being pulled to the floor and night lights being pulled from outlets to use the prongs to "draw" on the walls) and the more straightforward tearful trips to mom and dad's bed. This illustrates the point that what works for one family may not work for another family. As our car beds turned out not to be magical, we needed to implement some solid strategies to make the transition to big-kid beds smoother for everyone.

a 2:00 am party in their shared bedroom examining every nook and cranny of the room, as if they've never laid eyes on their own room before; run to mom and dad's bedside repeatedly, crying that they are scared; or a mixture of these. Such shenanigans do not lead to a good night's sleep!

In an ideal world, we would all have homes large enough to give each twin his own bedroom. However, most of us need our twins to share a bedroom for simple reasons of space. And with a shared bedroom comes all the fun of "monkey see, monkey do."

How do you make the transition to big-kid beds as smoothly as possible? Be realistic, and remember that no matter how prepared you are and how well you obey the rules of how to keep your kids in their own beds all night, your children are human and there will be some rough nights! Remember that the rough patches are just temporary road bumps, and if you follow the basic sleep rules consistently, your twins will once again be sleeping peacefully each night. Illness, travel, and schedule changes can all affect nighttime sleep; keep this in mind when having a particularly tiresome sleep week (pun intended!). "This too shall pass," and your kids will be on to the next milestone. And in a way, the process of training your toddler twins to stay in their big-kid beds all night is similar to training babies to sleep through the night.

Strategies to Survive

Now we will discuss some useful sleep strategies to use during the big-kid bed transition. First of all, when your twins are around the age of 2 years and are *not* quite climbing out of their cribs yet, I recommend placing a pressure-mounted gate in their bedroom doorway frame. Placing a gate at the doorway ahead of time will give your twins time to get used to the gate's presence while they are still comfortable in their familiar cribs. The gate will become part of the bedroom landscape and will play an important role when the big-kid beds are in place—keeping your twins *in* their bedroom, where they should be sleeping, and preventing them from running around the house, unencumbered, wreaking havoc with no limits. The gate is especially a good idea if you are a heavy sleeper—you might not even hear your twins escape into the kitchen at 4:00 am for a free-for-all.

Twin Tip!

A nice idea that may work if your twins share a large bedroom is to put the big-kid beds in the room while the cribs are still there. Have both cribs and both beds in the room at the same time for a couple of days, allowing some time to talk about the change, and you can give each child a choice as to where they want to sleep at night, in the crib or the new bed. Some kids are excited and adventurous and can't wait to try out the new bed. Other kids are a bit more hesitant and want to sleep in their familiar crib a bit longer. Both options are fine! The beauty of this method is that you are giving your twins the power to choose between 2 acceptable choices, and your children will feel empowered and more in control of the situation. At our house, our twin sons share a small bedroom that did not have the space to use this trick. So instead, we talked about the transition frequently and let the twins check out their older brother's bed—it got to a point where the twins were very ready and excited to use their new beds, and felt in control of the situation.

The next step is the selection of the new big-kid bed. Try to involve your twins in the process as much as possible. Discuss the transition often with your children. If there are older kids in the family, point out how the twins can be like their big brother or sister now. Let them explore the older sibling's bed. Look for children's books at your local library about getting a big-kid bed. These steps will help your twins emotionally prepare for the change.

If your big-kid beds don't have built-in sides, you'll need to make sure your kids don't roll out of bed while sleeping. I recommend pushing each bed into a corner of the bedroom and placing a single safety gate on the exposed side. Two gates are much more affordable than 4 safety gates to protect 4 open sides.

Another strategy for a smooth transition to big-kid beds is to keep every other aspect of the nighttime routine the same. Bath time, pajamas, story, bed—whatever your rituals are, keep doing them! Consistent evening rituals will reassure your twins that their entire worlds are not changing, just the bed on which they sleep.

When you tuck your twins in bed, remind them that nighttime is for sleeping. "When it's dark outside, we all sleep. When it's daytime and sunny, that's when we play." Be firm and leave the room. If the twins are not falling asleep or at least being quiet, wait for 10 or 15 minutes, and if necessary, check in on them to get them back in their beds. Don't give in to requests for you to lay with them unless you're prepared to spend the next 5 years sleeping on their bedroom floor. Use the same methods that you used when the twins were 3 months old—check in on them, be nonchalant and businesslike, tell them to sleep in their beds, and leave the room.

If your twins have a hard time settling at night you may need to start sleep success sticker calendars, one for each twin, to monitor their progress and teach them what to strive for. A night where each child falls asleep quietly earns one sticker on that calendar date. After 5 stickers, for example, the child earns a small prize (your local dollar store is a perfect place to choose such a prize). Start with a low number of stickers to earn a prize to give each child a taste of success, and then raise the bar, increasing the number of stickers to earn a prize as your twins learn acceptable sleep behavior.

If your twins start waking each other and you up in the middle of the night, be businesslike and march them back to their beds as many times as necessary.

Twin Tip!

You may be surprised to have just one twin waking up a lot, while her sister sleeps peacefully through all the noise. If this happens, be grateful that only one child is awakening, and encourage her to lie quietly in her bed and fall asleep so as not to disturb her sister.

Nighttime awakenings may need to be incorporated into the success sticker charts—each twin earns a sticker for a full night's sleep. I've noticed that when I use success sticker charts with my twin boys, competition sets in and the boys are very eager to do well and earn more stickers. A little friendly competition can be a good thing if it will help everyone sleep through the night again!

Twin Tip!

You'll need to evaluate each twin's overall sleep pattern if rough nighttime patterns emerge. Make sure that afternoon naps do not extend past 4:00 pm so as not to interfere with nighttime sleep.

The Need for Naps, or at Least Quiet Time

Later on in the toddler years, when your twins are about to turn 3 years old and have big-kid beds, it will be a challenge for them to settle down for an early afternoon nap. But if your toddlers are approaching their third birthday and resisting afternoon naps, don't just eliminate naps cold turkey! Transition the early afternoon nap into an hour of enforced quiet time to replace the nap time. Quiet time is an hour where everyone rests quietly, the television is off, and maybe one twin decides to look through a book while the other examines her right foot for a while. Quiet time can happen in the twins' bedroom, mom and dad's bedroom, the family room, or whatever location works for you—it can even switch locations as need be. The important thing is for your twins to simply relax and rest before continuing on with the rest of the day.

Twin Tip!

A break from a hectic schedule to rest is always a healthy idea, whether you are a child or an adult! If there's a younger baby in your home, coordinate quiet time with the baby's nap time. If there are older kids in the house, have your quiet time the hour before the older kids return home from school or encourage the older kids to have their own quiet time to read or play with toys. An hour of peace and quiet is always precious!

Each twin is an individual, and one twin may still be napping well while the other is clearly finished with daytime naps. In this situation, get creative. Let the napping twin nap alone in her room so she is not disturbed, and take her twin into your bedroom for an hour of quiet time.

Nutrition and Mealtimes

Feeding toddler twins can be a true adventure! You have 2 unique individuals on your hands. These individuals have different appetites at different times. Each twin may have different skills when learning how to self-feed, and they may have different taste preferences as well. How do you handle accommodating your unique kids' nutritional needs?

After the first birthday most healthy twins can drink vitamin D whole milk. Your twins should drink whole milk from 12 months until they turn 2 years old. Whole milk has a higher fat content than 2% or skim, which is important for your twins' still-developing brain and spinal cord. After the second birthday your twins can drink 2% or skim milk.

Whole milk, and all regular cow's milk, are a poor source of iron. Many kids have been known to fill up on milk and have a smaller appetite for nutrient-dense table foods, so keep track of how much milk your toddler twins are drinking each day. Your target amount of milk for each child is 16 to 20 ounces a day (not

Twin Tip!

Parents of twins always have a twin available for comparison—you need to remind yourself that everyone is an individual. Just because one of your kids happens to be hungry that day, do not feel the need to force-feed the twin who has a normal appetite! All too often we parents don't feel that we're doing a good job if our kids aren't eating 3 perfect square meals each day, but when you have toddlers, you need to relax. In the long run, you want to avoid recurring battles at mealtimes. Don't stress too much over one individual meal at a time; a meal may not have enough vegetables, for example, but the goal is healthful eating over 2 or 3 days taken as a whole.

more than 24 ounces in a day, which would increase the risk of iron deficiency anemia).

Feeding toddler twins is tough enough—avoid power struggles. If one twin is indicating that he is finished with his meal, end his meal. He may say "no," shove the spoon away, or throw his sippy cup—these are all signs that you should end his meal. Do not be tempted to keep feeding with tactics such as airplane spoons looking for a runway, or dancing spouses behind your head. Don't worry if his twin is still eating! Trust each of your twins' satiety center that tells them that their tummy is full.

Appropriate portion sizes at mealtime can be surprising to parents. A proper meal is a lot smaller than one may think, especially compared with the overly abundant serving sizes at restaurants today. A serving of fruit or vegetables is 1 tablespoon per year of the child's age. A serving of protein (for example, chicken, meats) is about the same size as your child's fist.

Twin Tip!

Avoid choking hazards—hot dogs, raw baby carrots, nuts, and whole grapes, for example. Make sure you slice food items lengthwise and into small pieces so they do not block your child's airway if accidentally inhaled.

You may notice that your twins have a smaller appetite as toddlers. Remember that your twins, and all children this age, are starting to slow down their rate of growth. The growth rate in the first year of life is astounding, and if the child kept that up for a few more years, he would soon be 9 feet tall! Because the child is not growing quite so quickly, he simply won't have the desire to eat as much as he did a few months earlier.

Serve finger foods to your toddlers, and introduce spoons and forks. Giving your twins more opportunities to self-feed is very challenging in the short run (and gets quite messy), but you'll make your family's life easier in the long run by starting utensil training early. Self-feeding is difficult for some parents to teach their kids, especially if you're a neat person! On a rushed morning, it may seem

Twin Tip!

Enjoy mealtime as a family, even when your twins are toddlers. To simplify life, families sometimes feed young twins dinner earlier in the evening, and the grown-ups eat later. And let's face it, some days can be crazy and you have to do what it takes to survive the week! However, a family meal at least twice a week will show your twins how to enjoy mealtimes and how to socially interact during the experience. Your toddler twins learn a lot by mimicking. It may seem like more work initially, but you'll see that the twins will begin to learn table manners by sitting with their families at mealtimes. Your twins will love spending the special time with you; they find you more fascinating than you would ever imagine!

easier to simply spoon-feed the cereal to your twins—you know that they're getting the nutrition they need, and it's faster, right? But on a less-harried morning, do give your kids a chance to try to scoop that cereal into their own mouths. With practice, they'll soon get there—imagine how much simpler life will be when they can feed themselves an entire meal. I felt as though my twin boys would never master getting the spoonful of food into their mouths—not only did they figure it out, but I found them feeding each other on a few occasions!

Twin Tip!

Each child's satiety center tells her when her tummy is full of food. Our kids are more aware of how full their stomachs are than we are—and when we allow our kids to *self*-feed, they will truly eat what they need. If they're not eating much, don't sweat it! They'll make up for it at the next meal.

Are you still concerned that your kids aren't eating well enough? Then ask yourself these questions.

- Are the twins growing appropriately, as measured at their well-child checkups?
- Are they having regular bowel movements, ideally once a day, but at least once every 2 to 3 days?
- Do the kids urinate regularly?

If your twins are peeing well, pooping well, and growing well, trust that they are eating well enough. Relax at mealtimes, help your twins learn to feed themselves, and continue to offer a variety of healthy choices for meals and snacks.

Are you concerned that your toddler twins are picky eaters and not eating a proper *variety* of foods? Continue to offer a variety of tastes and textures each day. Model an adventurous palate by eating a healthy variety yourself. Never declare your own finicky food preferences to your kids—if you refuse to eat certain foods, of course your kids will follow suit! You can discuss the issue with your pediatrician—a daily age-appropriate multivitamin may help parents feel better about their twins' nutritional status, and relax at mealtimes.

Twin Tip!

When you're feeding toddler twins day in, day out, remember to relax and keep your poker face on. If your kids see that they can get a rise out of you, whether it's a positive or negative reaction, they'll try again to get that reaction out of you!

Simplify Mealtime

Parents of toddler twins can simplify life by getting rid of their bib collection. I found that after the first birthday, messy meals never quite landed perfectly on a bib, rendering the bib somewhat useless. A spaghetti dinner with tomato sauce ends up on sleeves, in hair, and on pants. When your twins are learning how to self-feed, you can be sure food won't land on just the bib. Relax during mealtimes and don't fret if the kids are getting messy. Keep an extra stash of clothes near the kitchen for a quick change, if yogurt happened to find its way all over your twins' sleeves or got dumped in their laps. When an enormous stash of bibs is given away, there is a drawer now free and available to store something new.

Another mealtime change that makes life easier for parents of twins is changing infant high chairs to booster seats. Most kids around the age of 2 years are ready to sit still for a meal and are balanced enough to not fall out of their chair. Every child is an individual, however, and if one or both of your twins tends to run away from the dinner table immediately, or doesn't have the best sense of balance, then hold onto those high chairs a bit longer. Our family used wonderful toddler feeding seats that are placed on regular

Twin Tip!

The home of a family with twins runs more smoothly when everyone has regular bowel habits! It is pretty common for toddlers to experience occasional constipation. Switching to cow's milk and having varied eating patterns (eating like a horse one day, eating like a bird the next) can have its effects on a toddler's bowel movements. Make sure your twins are not drinking too much cow's milk, which could make the constipation worse—no more than 20 ounces a day. Offer plenty of fresh fruits and vegetables at every opportunity. If you have picky toddlers, keep experimenting until you find a fiber-rich food that they love that keeps their bowels moving and their mouths happy. You can try oatmeal, or steamed baby carrots softened and sliced lengthwise, for example. My kids adore mangoes, a very fiber-rich and nutritious fruit. Fresh apples or pears are great, and for convenience, keep canned fruits on hand such as pear, apricot, or peach. The canned fruits tend to be nice and mushy and easy for a toddler's mouth to handle. When you find a high-fiber food that your twins love, make a mental note of it and use it as your magic bullet when you notice that constipation is starting to set in.

dining chairs. They are slip-proof, made of a comfortable foam material, do not have complicated straps, are pretty straightforward for a child to climb into and out of, and are easy to wipe clean (or stick in the sink for a deeper cleaning). An added bonus to switching to boosters: they are more streamlined and will reduce the visual clutter in your dining area.

⋧ The Importance of Positive One-on-one Time

A child's toddler years are particularly interesting because it is the period that she is evolving into an actual person. Sure, different infants have different temperaments and personalities, but after the first birthday your twins are truly becoming little people. They're not just feeding and burping machines anymore! Spending quality one-on-one time with each twin every day is important during this critical stage.

How is it possible to have daily quality time with each child if you have twins and perhaps other children in your family? It is ideal for you to spend quality time with each of your children each day, whether they are a twin or singleton. There are different strategies for squeezing in quality special time depending on the situation.

If it is the weekend and your spouse is home, take one of your twins with you to the grocery store or on errands. Her twin can have special time with her other parent at home. Grocery shopping is something that must be accomplished each week. Multitask and combine the necessary errand with special time with your child. While you're at the store together, point out the colors of the apples you are choosing. Count out loud as you put each apple in a bag. Buying apples may seem mundane to you, but to a 21-month-old who usually has to share her mom with her twin, who rarely gets mom all to herself, well, buying apples can be a real blast!

On days when mom and dad are home, you don't even need to leave the house to get individual special time with your kids. One parent can take one twin out to the yard while the other parent reads with the other twin. One twin can play upstairs with mom while the other twin colors downstairs with dad. Make it a natural part of your household routine to occasionally separate the twins. Remind

> ## *Twin Tip!*
>
> If you have to buy stamps at the post office, visit the bank, or even fill up at the gas station, bring just one of your twins with you. Ignore your cell phone and simply *be* with your child. Your child will find the trip fascinating; at this age, children do not need a theme park or a toy store to get excited!

yourself to not simply think of your twins as a unit that cannot be split up.

If your spouse works extended hours, be sure to ask grandparents, family, and friends for assistance. See if Grandma can stay with one twin for an hour while you take his twin out. Think creatively and you'll find ways to squeeze in more quality time. Whether your twins are split up between mom and dad or mom and Aunt Jen, each child will get a chunk of time to feel special and have an adult all to herself. Everyone wins!

Some stressful days, to be honest, all I wanted to do was escape *alone* to the grocery store, just to think clearly and get a break from the house routine and demands. And definitely, if you feel the need

> ## *Twin Tip!*
>
> When we squeeze in special one-on-one time with each of our twins, these are the moments that we hoped to experience when we decided to become parents in the first place. These moments are what parenthood is all about! You're not just feeding and changing diapers, you're really *communicating* with your child in a meaningful way. With a busy house full of kids, sometimes we lose sight of that, and we need to remember to figure out what makes each kid tick. When you afford yourself the luxury of being in the company of just one of your kids alone, you have the pleasure of getting to know just who this little person is!

to run an errand *by yourself* for the sake of preserving your sanity, you should do so. But it may surprise you to see how easy it is to take just *one* child with you to a store! Living with twins each day, you take for granted how hard you're working raising 2 or more kids. If you take just one child on an outing, you'll think to yourself, wow, only one kid to take care of! The special time not only benefits your child, it benefits you as a parent as well. You'll have special moments with your twin that will show you who your child is becoming.

How can you squeeze in one-on-one time during a busy day when you don't have the help of a second adult to care for the other twin? Look for opportunities throughout the day, and take advantage of them. Is one of your 24-month-old twins occupying himself by looking through a book? Drop what you're doing and quietly join the other twin and work on a puzzle together for a few moments. Let the laundry sit there—it will still be there later! Any chunk of time spent together meaningfully is beneficial. If the twin interrupts 3 minutes into the puzzle project, it's no big deal. In terms of balance between the twins' special time, you can steal a moment of quality time with the other twin later on.

Obviously you'll want a balance; make sure you're spreading the special time as evenly as possible between your twins. But remember that your twins will never have *exactly* the same amount of one-on-one time with you. It's impossible, and that's OK! You're aiming to be *fair,* but you can never make their experiences perfectly equal. If you notice that one twin has been acting out more frequently, try increasing your positive one-on-one time with him. You'll see an improvement in his behavior as a result.

🐦 Kind But Effective Discipline

Good discipline starts with good communication. When you want to communicate well with someone, whether it is your child, your spouse, a coworker, or a boss, you should look the person in the eyes and convey that you are listening. Eye contact and engagement go a long way to ensure that the person you are speaking with feels validated in what he is trying to say. Above all, each of your twins wants you to be engaged with her.

Twin Tip!

If you are squeezing in at least 15 minutes of one-on-one time a day with each child, you are doing well! Many refer to this special time as *time-in* (to differentiate it from a time-out). Providing each twin with plenty of time-in will earn you better behavior from your children in the long run. Kids who feel respected, loved, and listened to will not be so desperate for attention that they will misbehave to get negative attention. Sprinkle lots of positive attention on each of your twins each day, specific to who each child is as an individual, and your twins will feel more emotionally secure and behave better.

Parents of twins have the challenge of 2 young kids at the same age, often pulling a parent in 2 different directions. Even though it can be hectic with twins in your home, give your best effort each day to truly listen to each child during pleasant interactions. Each of your twins will have a deeper connection to you, and when the time comes that your child does something she should not, your response as a parent illustrates a clear difference between appropriate and inappropriate behavior. Good communication is the backbone of effective discipline.

Twin Tip!

When we discuss proper methods to discipline toddler twins, we need to define what discipline really means. Discipline does not mean the same thing as punishment. When I refer to proper discipline, I am referring to an overall household framework where good behavior is rewarded and unacceptable behavior has appropriate consequences. Discipline takes into consideration lots of positive quality time with your child, and then dictates that poor behavior eliminates any kind of attention.

Acceptable Choices and Listening

Give your twins plenty of opportunities each day to make acceptable choices. "Would you like the orange cup or the blue cup?" "Would you like the butterfly shirt or the one with the hearts on it?" Help your twins feel empowered in daily interactions by letting them select between 2 acceptable alternatives.

Above all, your toddler twins want to be heard. Your twins want to know that you love them and respect them as individuals. When your 20-month-old twins start shrieking for their sippy cups, you should calmly ask them, "What do you need? Do you want your cup? Can you ask nicely please?" You may not feel patient enough every day to have this conversation, but if you remain calm, your children will follow suit.

Twin Tip!

If you feel your blood pressure rising with your toddler twins' demands, you can use some tricks to keep your cool. Imagine that you have an audience in the room with you, watching you interact with your twins, and you'll find yourself saying the right things even though you didn't think you could. Or, you can pretend that your twins are from another country and you're slowly introducing them to your language. These ideas may sound a bit silly, but it is key that you keep your cool and remain calm when disciplining your twins, even if you need to use a gimmick to do so!

Make the effort to coach your toddler twins to use their words and language instead of more barbaric behaviors. Even at this early age, if you give your child milk each time he *cries* for it, you are essentially teaching him to yell every time he wants milk. Start coaching him now to calm down and express himself politely.

Encourage good behavior when your twins are toddlers, rather than waiting and having more poor behavior to fix later. In the case of toddler twins, you are coaching 2 kids how to be civilized at the

Twin Tip!

Parents of twins, listen up. Communication and relationships are a two-way street. Just as you expect your kids to
listen to and respect your house rules, you need to give
your kids the courtesy of listening to and respecting them
as well. To develop trust, avoid making empty promises.
As an example, if you promise your child a trip to the
playground after visiting the library, make sure you follow
through on your promise. If you are consistent and your
kids trust you, and they know you will do what you *said*
you would do, your children will be calmer and more
patient on the whole.

same time—a lot of work, but you will reap the rewards in the long
run. If you are reaching your limit (and who isn't reaching their limit
when dealing with 2 sweet but at times emotional toddlers?), take
a moment, catch your breath, and react as consistently as you can.
You won't be the perfect parent every day, but if you can do the right
thing 80% of the time you're doing pretty well.

Address what your child is saying to you. Acknowledge his
feelings. "You're upset, aren't you? Do you wish we were going to the
playground? I'm sorry we don't have time for that today; we need to
go home and have lunch now." If one twin is getting hysterical about
something, his twin may pick up on the madness and escalate the
situation. When both twins are starting to lose their cool, calmly call
a meeting to order. Get down to your twins' eye level. Talk in a low,
calm voice. Use every fiber in your being to not lose *your* cool! "We
do not yell in our house. Please use your words. Dad said that it is
bath time, and that means we are going to take our baths now."

Temper Tantrums

If one or both of your twins truly start to melt down into a temper
tantrum, you need to ignore the hysterics. Just make sure that your
child is safe and won't hurt himself or anyone else during the tantrum, and let him scream. You don't want to reward a tantrum with

bribes, pleading, or any kind of attention—unless you would like to have more tantrums in your house on a daily basis, that is!

Consistency Is Key

Be consistent with your house rules every day, even on days when you're exhausted. I think that this is the most challenging aspect of good discipline. Sure, we all know to be consistent and have the same expectations of our kids' behavior each day…but in the real world, when the twins were up all night with colds and you are about to pass out from fatigue, guess what? You've still got to be on your A game when it comes to parenting! Whether you're having a great day or a bad day, you still need to be consistent with your house rules so that your toddler twins learn that the rules exist no matter what day of the week it is.

I like using the term *house rule* with my kids because it removes the individuals from the rule. A house rule is simply the way the world works. Rules are not about what mom wants, or what your twin wants; the rules are just the way it is. When my parents babysit our kids, they appreciate the idea of house rules, as grandparents tend to not like to be the bad guy—they can avoid taking any blame in their grandchildren's eyes by saying, "We don't bang on the window—that's a house rule!"

Twin Tip!

Your twins may test you when family and friends come for a visit, or when you go to a party, to see if your reaction will be the same. Don't slack on the rules just because you are socializing! Toddlers are very smart and if you let your guard down on a house rule just once or twice, they will remember it like an elephant and challenge you on it repeatedly.

Time-outs

Once your children are around the age of 2 years, they are starting to sense what is right or wrong. You and your spouse should discuss privately what should be considered behavior that will not be tolerated (hitting or biting, for example). Both parents and caregivers need to be on the same page when it comes to proper discipline. If one of the twins hits the other, for example, declare a time-out immediately, without delay. You need to connect the offense with the punishment for your child. The offending twin should go to a boring part of the room with no toys (we used a plain corner) and sit alone 1 minute for each year of age. If your twin tries to escape time-out, silently march her right back. The whole idea of time-out is to remove all fun and attention.

> ## *Twin Tip!*
> Disciplining toddlers can be very frustrating. Remind yourself that this is a difficult stage and you *will* get past it! Often your twins may refuse to stay in their designated time-out location. Your toddler twins may really fight you on going to time-out, but if you are consistent with your rules, you will see improvement over time. Hang in there!

Avoid the urge to yell, however mad you may truly be. Attention is attention even if it is unpleasant and negative. Twins, as opposed to single-born kids, especially crave their parent's attention, and they may actually enjoy being yelled at (on a certain level) because they've got their parent's complete attention all to themselves. So remember—time-outs are effective only if they are used properly, meaning removing all fun and attention. When the time-out period is up (an egg timer is handy), calmly get down to your child's eye level and explain why she got the time-out. Hug and move on with the day.

If a highly desirable new toy or object is causing repeated fighting, you have 2 options. Option 1—get an egg timer and give each child a 4-minute turn with the item, and then alternate turns for each twin (adjust the timing as necessary). If the fighting is really bad, use option 2—give the toy itself a time-out. Your twins need to learn that if they can't share and play nicely with something, *no one* gets to play with it. Hide it well and try again the next day if the twins are better behaved.

> ## *Twin Tip!*
> What do you do when *both* twins have violated house rules? What do you do when both twins are hitting each other in a fight over a new truck toy? Do not ask, "Who started it?" If you ask who started it, it will teach your toddlers how to start blaming each other. And does it really matter who started it when they are now both hitting? They *both* need a time-out away from each other—plan out 2 areas ahead of time for just this occasion. The last thing you need at this point is a fight over who gets which time-out location. How can you keep 2 kids in 2 different time-out spots? Is there a hallway in your home in which you can create a confined area with a temporary pressure-mounted gate? Brainstorm to see if you can create 2 safe zones for time-out sessions.

Essentially, your toddler twins are like scientists in a real-life laboratory. They perform behavioral experiments by acting differently in certain situations. They observe your reaction to their behavior and any resulting consequences, and register the information in their data files. If you consistently give positive attention for good behavior and remove all fun and attention for bad behavior, your twins' data files will help them make the right decisions down the line. You will have to live through a frustrating couple of years of continued research so they can verify their findings, but if you and your spouse provide a consistent framework of discipline, your scientists will emerge from toddlerhood with better manners for it!

ꙮ Encouraging Language Development

Toddlers improve their language skills by directly talking with the people in their world, as well as by observing other people in their world speak with one another. The most beneficial thing you can do as a parent to get your twins talking is to simply speak with each of them, a lot. Narrate your lives together. "Here comes the shampoo. Let's scrub your head! Rinse with water. The water is warm and

Twin Tip!

I must warn you about self-fulfilling prophecies—if you expect a certain kind of behavior from your twins, you are likely to get it. I have often heard parents say, "Oh well, boys will be boys," for example, letting their sons get away with more than they should. Along those same lines, there seems to be a preconceived idea of twins as being mischievous (sayings such as "double trouble" come to mind)—but you need to be aware of what your mind-set is. If you simply throw up your hands and say, "Oh well, they're twins, I guess they're supposed to give me a hard time," you may end up slacking on their daily discipline. Make sure you expect the best behavior out of both of them, as if they were each single-born children. If you are inconsistent, you'll end up with twins who are hard to handle. If you have high expectations for your twins and are consistent with them, you will be rewarded.

wet!" Surround your twins with words to help them learn how to use the words.

Many people believe in a secret twin language that only your pair of twins understands. Personally, I feel that there isn't a secret language so much as the fact that one twin will say a word the wrong

Twin Tip!

In the early talking years, some parents find mispronounced words or brand-new, made-up words to be incredibly sweet and adorable! These early words are cute—make sure that you record the invented words in each twin's respective baby book, and laugh about it at night with your spouse when the twins are sleeping. But in the presence of your twins, repeat the *correct, real* word back with exaggerated enunciation to help them learn. Don't perpetuate repetition of incorrect words, even if they're really funny.

> ## *Twin Tip!*
>
> Do you have boy-boy or girl-girl twins? Help extended family and friends identify who is who. Dress your twins in distinctive clothing and teach them how to introduce themselves. "Hi, I'm Ryan." Your toddler twins, still quite young, probably don't realize that others can confuse them with one another. Helping each of your twins tell loved ones who they are will minimize others' tendency to regard your twins as a unit and encourage the understanding that they are 2 separate individuals.

way, and his twin will understand what he meant to say, and then the two of them continue to reuse the wrong pronunciation of the word. For example, "milk" is spoken "moak," and soon enough both twins are calling it "moak." If this happens, be supportive of your twins' attempts to talk, and repeat the correct word. "You would like miiiilk? OK, I'll pour you more miiiilk." Place emphasis on the correct pronunciation. Avoid saying negative things to the effect of, "No, that's not how you say it," inadvertently shaming your toddlers from attempting to say new words. Just keep repeating the correct words until the twins catch on.

On the whole, twins' language development can take a bit longer compared with that of their single-born peers, simply because they are usually sharing the same caregivers. You can't have a one-on-one conversation with each twin at the same time! Just do your best and the twins will catch up; usually by 4 or 5 years of age, twins are talking as clearly as their peers. If you have specific concerns about one or both twins, check with your pediatrician. Don't be surprised if just one of the twins needs a language boost with some speech therapy.

Toilet Training—Is It Possible?

Imagine, if you dare, a new world in which you're not changing diapers all day long! In this magical new land, you don't have to stock up on diapers every time you leave the house! Do you dare to dream?

Believe it or not, it will happen. Your twins will indeed wear underwear one day, and they'll keep their underwear clean and dry! When will this happen? The timing of toilet training is up to your twins, ultimately, with mom and dad's encouragement and involvement. Toileting success may not happen as early as it did for your neighbor's kid, and it may not happen by the time your niece was wearing underwear, but don't worry—it will happen. The age of a child when toilet trained has no bearing on that child's future intelligence or status in the world! Early toilet trained kids don't all attend Harvard; they were trained early because they had exceptional personal interest in the potty, had highly motivated and available parents willing and able to intensely train them, or a mix of the two.

And that's the key, isn't it? We're not just talking about training 1 child, but 2! You can do it! Toilet training doesn't happen overnight; let's back up a bit and discuss the ages and stages that are involved.

When and Where Do We Start?

Start talking about the toileting process with your twins at around 18 months of age. Nothing intense here; we're just talking about starting to define terms (for example, pee, poop, potty, flush) and introducing the topic. When one of your twins poops in his diaper, use it as an opportunity to talk about potty training. If you see him straining to poop, say, "It looks like you're pooping in your diaper! Good job!" This way he'll learn the word for what it is he is doing.

Even if you are self-conscious, I recommend an open-door policy when it comes to using the bathroom in the privacy of your own home. When you need to visit the bathroom yourself, let your twins see what happens. How will they learn if they've never seen anyone

Twin Tip!

Always be positive and upbeat about the toileting process. Toileting is a normal and natural phenomenon—*Everyone Poops,* after all, just as Taro Gomi's well-known children's book is titled! Resist the urge to wrinkle your nose at even the stinkiest of diapers—it is important for your twins to know that pooping is healthy and normal.

else do it? Older siblings (if they don't mind) are also useful in this regard. So much can be learned by mimicking others! Anyway, when you have toddler twins in your house, you're being followed around all day as it is; so let them learn what that big mysterious toilet is there for.

You can step toilet training up a bit around the age of 24 months. Certainly, if your twins are very eager to learn, showing the signs of readiness, and perhaps trying to be more like their older sibling, you can intensify the process sooner. Just be prepared to back off a bit if one or both of your twins are showing signs of resistance. Any power struggles will only lengthen the overall process and will really test your stamina. But around 24 months, most kids are showing signs of true readiness, including walking well to a potty, positioning themselves on the potty properly without losing balance, speaking well enough to use the proper terms, and having stronger bladder and bowel control (so as to hold it to run to the potty in time). Are your twins' diapers still dry after 2 or 3 hours? That's a good sign!

Helpful Gear

Invest in 2 potty chairs, or one potty chair and a ring to place on the adult toilet seat. These could also be borrowed to save some money; ask your family and friends if they can give you their old ones. A good slip-proof step stool will help too. I had hoped that my twin boys would be eager to sit on a ring on the real toilet, as their big brother did, reducing cleanup work for me. Unfortunately, they were afraid to sit so high up; they preferred to be lower to the ground. So we had 2 identical potties (to avoid bickering over who got which seat) and kept them handy wherever we were spending time. In the daytime we were mostly downstairs, so we placed the 2 potties in

Twin Tip!

Stock up on children's books about using the potty, by buying them or borrowing them from others or the local library. Reading plenty of these potty books will help ingrain the idea in your twins' heads and promote the whole idea. I liked to refer to it as potty "brainwashing."

our main hallway (great for decorating, let me tell you), as we didn't have enough room in the bathroom for both potties. Always having a potty nearby is not so fun, but it does help your toddlers remember them and find them easily if they get the urge to pee. We'd bring the 2 potties with us upstairs in the evening, so they were close at hand when giving baths and getting ready for bed.

Schedule Potty Time Into Your Day

Start scheduling potty time once a day—a chunk of time each day when the twins sit on their potties to practice, regardless of any result. Choose a quiet time that works for your schedule so that everyone is relaxed. Make potty time fun—read books together, sing songs, and heap on the positive attention. If you like and are able, you can give each twin her own potty time so that she gets your full attention. The kids can initially sit on the potty chair with their clothes still on, so that they get used to the idea, but soon they can take their diapers off. You're aiming for 5 or 10 minutes of pleasant practice time together. If your twins want to keep sitting longer, great, and if they run off after a couple of minutes, that's OK too. We're not looking for actual results right now; the idea of potty time is to learn that sitting on the potty is something we do every day.

Don't force the potty time or engage in a power struggle over it. If one or both twins defiantly do not want to sit on their potty chair, back off and try again another day, or experiment with another time such as before the afternoon nap. You'll eventually work your way up to holding potty time 2 times a day.

Is one twin clearly more interested in the potty than the other? Many parents of twins prefer to train their kids one at a time. This seems to work well particularly for boy-girl twins, as girls seem to be interested in toilet training earlier than boys, on average.

Depending on your comfort level and the degree of success you're seeing at potty time, you can make a big production out of selecting some big-kid underwear at the store. Now you can start having underwear time each day, starting with a couple of hours' worth and increasing from there. In our house, we had our underwear time every afternoon starting from after the afternoon nap to bath time before bed. Every hour of underwear time, check in with each twin to ask if he needs to use the potty, "to keep your underwear clean and dry."

Motivation Tools

Success sticker charts, or potty charts, work really well for toilet training and really help kids to feel special! You can buy 2 big, blank poster boards at the store—have each twin choose a distinct color—and hang the posters in a central location of your home where everyone can see them clearly.

Make a big production out of writing each twin's name at the top of each poster, and draw a row of small squares at the top. Start small and make this first row only 3 squares long. Each square will get filled with a sticker (1 sticker for peeing on the potty; 2 stickers for pooping on the potty—small reward sticker collections are easily found at discount stores) and when the row of squares is filled with stickers, the child can choose a small prize. The first row should be short so that your child can have an early taste of success, and the following rows can have progressively more squares to raise the bar.

Twin Tip!

Our sons' potty charts were taped to the side of our kitchen island. Displayed potty charts are not going to be the next great idea in the world of kitchen design, but potty training is a temporary situation, and our boys could watch their progress unfold at eye level in a central location in our home, encouraging them toward more success.

Some families use candy rewards during the toilet training process; however, as a pediatrician, I would warn against this. Food rewards, even if given with good intentions, can unfortunately send an unhealthy message to your kids by fostering an attitude about treats that can contribute to weight problems in the future. The potty charts may require a bit more effort than just handing out candy, but the beauty of the potty chart is that your kids can visualize all their success and see how far they've come. The charts can be a real confidence builder. See what works for your family.

Accidents will happen—expect them and be prepared for them so you are not caught off guard. Keep extra-absorbent cloths handy to help clean up accidents—burp cloths from the infancy days are great for this purpose. Have extra wet wipes handy. When accidents happen, do your best to keep your cool—remain calm and have your child help you clean up the accident by giving her an extra cloth to wipe the floor. Teach your twins to put their dirty pants in the laundry hamper *themselves*, and where to get clean pants themselves. You want each twin to understand how much easier and more pleasant it is to simply pee and poop in the potty. We kept a shelf nearby stocked with burp cloths, extra underwear, and extra pants just to make cleaning up after the inevitable accidents easier to handle.

Twin Tip!

Expect setbacks, and don't be discouraged by them. Illness, changes in the daily schedule, travel, a new baby—all can cause a temporary regression in toilet training. If your toddler twins have issues withholding painful poops and progressive constipation, consult with your pediatrician. Continue to be upbeat and positive, and your twins will recover. When you're really worried, just remember—they won't be attending high school in diapers. I promise!

Toilet training is truly complete when each child makes it to the potty in time with *no* reminders from a parent or caregiver. When you're seeing that your kids are doing well, try to back off on the reminders, so that they can learn to remind themselves.

Safety Issues

Continually reevaluate the childproofing in your home. Watch out for choking hazards that may have found their way into your twins' play areas. Your twins may be older now, but they may still decide to explore a small, unknown item by putting it in their mouths.

As your twins grow bigger their style of play changes—they are faster and stronger than when they were 13-month-olds. Two or more children chasing each other can get into more accidents than just one child playing alone. Are there hazards in your home that you didn't even realize were a problem? If a part of your home comes to your attention as unsafe, correct it before someone gets injured. When our twin boys were toddlers, they both fell on separate occasions, hitting the very same wall corner in a high traffic hallway—Ryan tripped into it, turning his forehead into one big bruised egg, and several months later, Andrew ran into it playing in an exciting game of hide-and-seek, splitting his upper lip. The day after Andrew received his stitches I purchased long foam cushions, made to childproof coffee tables, and taped them onto the wall corners in our high-traffic hallway. The padded-corner look may not appear in home decorating magazines anytime soon, but we rested a little easier knowing that lightning wouldn't strike at that spot a third time.

Twin Tip!

Playing outside in the yard can be very stressful for parents of toddler twins. The minute you go outside, one runs in one direction, and her twin runs in the completely opposite direction! Brainstorm different ways to enjoy the outdoors safely with your twins. Our backyard deck had openings to the beckoning yard, yet I wanted the option to have family meals outdoors. Our solution was to install child safety gates to block off the deck openings. The gates weren't aesthetically pleasing, but they were worth it to enjoy family dinners outdoors in nice weather, without worrying about 2 toddlers trying to escape. We ended up eating outdoors quite often with the luxury of the gates because cleanup of crumbs and spills is much easier outdoors!

Now that your twins are walking toddlers, you'll be spending more time outdoors. Teach your twins basic outdoor rules such as staying with a parent and not running into the street. A fenced-in yard is wonderful for containing your active toddler twins; if a fence is not an option, monitor your twins' locations diligently. Don't get a false sense of security when other adults are present—always make sure that both toddlers are being monitored when spending time outdoors.

⁊❧ Family Relationships—A New Baby?

Whether you plan it or not, another baby (or 2) may show up in the family, and it could be sooner than you think. Another baby in the house can be a challenge when the twins are mere toddlers themselves! Our twins were 28 months old when our fourth child was born—quite an adventure. I remember the hardest aspect of those initial months was trying to nurse the baby. The boys figured that when Mommy sat down to nurse the baby, they had the next 15 minutes to explore and wreak havoc—or so they thought. I had to get really creative to crack down on the madness, so that I could continue to nurse our baby girl. You can use special crayons, a new DVD, or a special rotating toy basket that is only brought out during baby's feeding time, to be quickly stored away again when nursing is complete so it doesn't lose its appeal. Have interesting activities for your toddler twins hidden away, and pull them out at critical times when you're busy with the baby.

Although those early months were difficult, we can see how far our twin boys have come since their baby sister's birth, and how much her presence in our family has helped them to grow up. Our twins are not the babies of the family—they are proud to show their sister how big kids do things. So if you find yourself pregnant again when your twins are still young, there are lots of positives that will result from the new family dynamic!

⁊❧ Keeping a Twin-Friendly Budget— Save Time and Money

As in the younger age groups, borrow as many clothes for your twins from family and friends as you can. Let everyone know that you gladly accept hand-me-down clothes. Don't worry if some items have small stains—save those pieces for home play days or as a change of pants during toilet training. Toddlers grow so fast that the borrowed items will soon be outgrown, and you'll be so glad you saved the money!

Shoes are an exception to the hand-me-down wardrobe. Every kid's feet are different (even identical twins) and every kid's walking pattern is slightly different, so brand-new shoes are preferable to mold to the feet and be shaped by walking patterns. Personally, I have made it a point to ask family and friends for their kids' old clothes, and the money that I saved by not buying new pants and shirts was diverted into buying new shoes. We have found some trusty, comfortable, reliable sneaker brands that are our standby day-to-day shoes; add a slightly dressier shoe and you're pretty much set for any occasion.

Twin Tip!

Try to buy your twins distinctive pairs of shoes; that way, each pair clearly belongs to a specific twin, and there is no squabbling over whose shoes are whose when rushing out the door. Using color themes for each child can extend to other items as well, such as drinking cups, to quickly identify whose cup is whose.

Your kids' shoes fit properly if there's a finger's breadth distance from the tip of the toes to the tip of the insole. When the kids' feet grow, we use our favorite Internet shoe store that has free shipping and free return shipping. We can confidently order the same brand and style of shoe, selecting a half size up, maybe getting new colors to be interesting. Because we know the shoe brand well I am confident that the new shoe will fit. I spend mere minutes ordering online, and a couple of days later the new shoes arrive on the doorstep. I find Internet shopping much easier on our lifestyle than schlepping toddler twins to various shoe stores, looking for something you like, hoping that the store will have the size you need in stock.

Internet shopping can be a real lifesaver. Many companies offer free shipping if you pay over a certain amount or will mail out

Twin Tip!

Figure out which Internet shopping sites have good deals on shipping. Save time, effort, and gas money, and spend an afternoon having fun instead of shopping. Take a neighborhood walk or hold a block-stacking competition! If you can streamline the mundane, routine, yet necessary tasks such as shoe shopping for ever-growing feet, you create more free time to enjoy your family.

special promotions for free shipping for a limited time—be on the lookout for these offers. You are too busy with 2 or more kids to be out shopping all the time!

🐾 Having Fun

All children love to listen to music and dance. Music is such a great tension reliever for kids *and* parents, and it's a great alternative to flipping on the television. Dance parties are a super fun way for toddler twins to let off energy and steam! Make sure you clear the floor of toys beforehand, as the dancing may get pretty wild! Excellent new kids' music has been coming out in recent years that is family friendly *and* fun for adults to listen to. It doesn't even have to be kids' music per se; early Beatles albums are pretty kid friendly, for example. Make sure the music you listen to is fun for you *all*. Your twins will notice when you really like a certain song and will enjoy hearing you sing along, even if you are tone deaf! Keep a stash of CDs in your car to listen to while running errands and driving on longer car trips.

Twin Tip!

Want to really have some fun with your toddler twins? Teach them the game of freeze dance, the classic where everyone must freeze like a statue when the music is paused. I guarantee a good time!

A word about the cleanliness of your home—don't worry about a messy house. Within reason, just let it go and play with your kids. Just make sure the floor isn't so cluttered that everyone's tripping everywhere! Your kids will not remember how clean the house was; they'll only remember the times that mom played fort with them using couch cushions, or when dad played garbage truck with them by compacting them with throw pillows. Soon enough the kids will grow older and you can clean the house as much as you want. Reserve power clutter-busting sessions for the evenings when the kids are in bed, so that the floor actually stays clear for a while, and you and your spouse can feel like normal people again, if just for a couple of hours.

Enjoy your twins, despite the challenges inherent in the toddler years, and watch with amazement how quickly they learn new things. Remember that the rough patches will last a limited amount of time, and then you'll move on to the next adventure!

❧ CHAPTER 7
The Preschool Years
(3- and 4-Year-Olds)

"*M*om, can you come to my restaurant?" "Daddy, would you read this book to me?" All of a sudden, your twins have grown into 2 wonderful people who can speak clearly and play cooperatively with each other as well as others! The preschool years with twins are truly magical. Three- and 4-year-olds burst with imagination. Not so long ago, your home was filled with constant feedings and frequent diaper changes. Now your home is a place where the couch is a train and a cardboard box is an airplane you can fly to the grocery store to buy a loaf of bread!

Relish these years and revel in playing like a child with your twins. Your preschool-aged twins want nothing more than a parent sitting on the floor with them, following along in a make-believe scenario that they are creating as you go along. Be a customer in one child's restaurant and order a banana split with extra ketchup on top. Help your other child play garbage truck by collecting assorted toys and dumping them at a garbage dump. Playtime serves a greater purpose than just fun—it is through imaginative play that 3- and 4-year-olds make sense of the world around them.

The possibilities of imaginative scenarios are limitless with 2 kids at the same creative age. You have 2 inventive minds bouncing ideas off each other. And conveniently, you have 2 actors to play out different roles—store cashier and shopper, pilot and copilot, or waiter and customer, for example.

Your twins are most likely wonderful playmates much of the time. However, do not expect your twins to play wonderfully with one another all the time, every day. Could you imagine being with the same person *all the time?* Two individuals with 2 minds of their own will have differing opinions from time to time! Disagreements between your twins are inevitable.

Is there a way to prevent inter-twin arguments from happening? Not in entirety, but there *is* a way to reduce the number of disagreements in your home. Giving each twin his own personal space is one way to prolong the peace in your home. If you respect the individual opinions and personal space of your twins, each will feel more self-assured, secure, and content. In this way, you can prevent some arguments from even starting.

Parents of preschool-aged twins notice that life is much easier than it was a couple of years earlier because twins can be such great playmates. However, keep in mind that your twins won't want to play together all the time, despite the convenience of such an arrangement for you as a parent. Each child needs her own distinct relationships with other siblings, relatives, and friends—all part of healthy and normal twin development. You'll notice different patterns emerging as one twin will buddy up with an older sibling frequently one month, while another month, the other twin will take great interest in a neighborhood friend, for example. As a parent of twins you want to encourage these budding outside relationships. Your twins will always have a unique and special twin bond, but early experiences with others will help socialize each twin as they embark on their school years. Such socialization is great for adjusting to a classroom setting. Much of the focus of the early school years is simply getting along with others and listening to instructions—your twins will be well prepared for school simply by socializing with the world around them.

Twin Tip!

Celebrate these wondrous preschool years with your twins. For the first couple of years, you synchronized your infant twins' schedules to make life more manageable. Now, at the preschool-aged stage of the game, parenting twins is less about daily survival and more about nurturing who each twin is as an individual.

Sleep Issues

Three- and 4-year-olds should be sleeping, on average, a total of 12 hours in a 24-hour period. Your twins may have given up their naps or, if bedtime is later or they've woken up early, they may take a quick 1- to 2-hour early afternoon nap. Expect a few months' time of an in-between phase—some days your twins may need the nap, and other days quiet time will suffice. As discussed in Chapter 6, encourage an hour of quiet time in the early afternoon. A restful break from the day's activities will help your twins be energized for the remainder of the day. Be creative with naps—one twin may like to keep napping while her twin doesn't need to. Allow one twin to nap in the shared bedroom while you read quietly with the twin in your bedroom, for example.

> ## *Twin Tip!*
>
> After the third birthday, you may notice that your twins nap well, but then resist bedtime. Experiment with your family's schedule to improve bedtime cooperation. You may decide to transition your 3-year-olds' naps into quiet time to ensure that they fall asleep easily at a consistent bedtime. However, if one or both parents work outside the home, you may need to continue afternoon naps until the age of 5 years to prevent your twins from being overtired at later bedtimes.

If your twins share a bedroom, one twin may wake the other twin too early in the morning. Encourage both twins to stay in bed if the sun hasn't come up yet—"When it's dark out, we sleep, and when it's light out, we can play." Teach your twins what to do in different situations; they're old enough now to understand what you expect of them. For example, teach them that if one wakes up and it's light outside, but the other is still sleeping, the twin who is awake should quietly tiptoe out of the room so as not to disturb the other. You'll likely have several mornings where one twin is bright eyed and bushy tailed, while her twin is still yawning with heavy eyelids. If you don't all have to leave the house that morning, encourage the sleepy twin to go back to bed, making a teaching point for the awake twin, so they can learn for the next time.

A great way to help ensure a good night's sleep is to make sure your twins get plenty of activity and exercise during the daytime. Your preschooler twins are naturally filled with energy! Getting lots of motion in during the day will help the twins be more restful at night. Playgrounds help kids exercise their large muscle groups by climbing and balancing. Neighborhood and nature walks get kids' legs moving, with short bursts of running sprinkled throughout. Get your twins practicing on tricycles, and advance to 12-inch bikes with training wheels once they're a bit taller. Don't forget the bike helmets! Make learning new physical activities fun, like a game. Simply running around the yard can provide great physical activity—you can play catch or monkey in the middle.

> ## Twin Tip!
> Keep your twins active each day to promote better quality nighttime sleep! Aim for at least 30 minutes a day of cumulative physical activity. The exercise still counts if it is done in smaller bursts scattered throughout the day.

In wintertime or during bad weather, you'll need to get creative to find ways to get your twins' bodies moving and hearts pumping. Clear out your play area for a safe game of catch with a soft ball, or play hide-and-seek. Our family cleared the space in our unfinished basement, cushioned wall corners and sharp edges, and kept the boys' bikes there all winter. Many afternoons we'd head downstairs so the boys could strap on their bike helmets and have a ball riding their bikes around while it was freezing cold outside. See what fun ideas you can come up with to squeeze in daily physical activity to help your twins sleep more solidly at night.

✿ Socialization—The Twins' Role Within the Family

Your 3-year-old twins are eager to learn about the world around them. When kids have a strong sense of their role within a family, they more easily navigate through their lives, at all ages. How can a 3-year-old feel like part of a family? Enlist their help around the house. Taking care of the home is not just a parent's job; it is *every* family member's responsibility, and you can exercise the philosophy starting at a young age.

Preschool-aged kids *love* to help with housework. Give your twins dust cloths to clean off tabletops while you vacuum. Sorting laundry? Make a pile of the twins' underwear and have one child put the clean underwear back in the proper drawer (teach your kids where everything goes). The other child can pair socks together to put in the sock drawer. Coaching your kids to perform simple housework tasks may seem like more work initially, but the rewards are worth the effort. Your twins will learn quickly, and soon you will see that they *really* are helping. Besides, daily mundane house chores are more fun when tackled as a team!

> ## *Twin Tip!*
> Discount stores have nice-looking nonbreakable dinnerware (usually intended for outdoor entertaining)—have a set on hand, and your twins can help set the table each night without fear of broken dishes.

When your twins help with household chores, the job doesn't have to be performed perfectly. Applaud each child's *effort,* not the outcome. Chores help each twin feel like a contributing member of the family, which will go a long way to boosting his self-esteem. The bonus for you—a 3-year-old who is accustomed to helping around the house will grow into an older child who helps around the house! Expect each child to help at a young age so that it becomes a natural part of everyone's routine. Eight-year-olds won't magically start tidying up their bedrooms on their own without having had some prior experience.

The most important job your twins can help with is keeping the toy clutter under control. Multiple young children in one single home can quickly result in a crowded floor of random toys. Coach your twins to put away toys when they are finished playing with them. Big baskets and totes can simplify the process. Cars go in one basket, trains in another basket, and stuffed animals in a third basket, for example.

We're not looking for perfect organization from 3-year-olds. We're simply sending the message that when you're done playing with

> ## *Twin Tip!*
> Borrow an organization strategy from preschool teach-ers—take digital pictures of each toy group and print the pictures on your home printer. Tape the pictures to storage bins so that nonreaders can check the picture to see what goes where.

something, you should pick up after yourself. Make cleanup fun and set an egg timer for 3 minutes—have a speed cleanup race to see how much can be put away before the timer goes off. Once everyone gets in the habit of helping clean up, it becomes part of the daily routine.

> ## *Twin Tip!*
> Organization in your twins' closet can streamline your morning routine. Choosing one's own clothes to wear each day will help your twins feel like they have some control over their daily lives. Organize your twins' clothing into groups of play clothes or nicer clothes. Depending on the day's activities, you can instruct your twins to dress themselves in play clothes, for example, if you are all headed to a neighborhood playground. Your children get a sense of ownership by having a choice, and they are still dressed appropriately for the occasion.

Your twins will learn to interact with the outside world by getting lots of practice at home interacting with family members. Age-appropriate board or card games are a great way to teach social skills while getting in some good family bonding time. Your twins will learn to take turns and have fun whether they win or lose. Younger twins may have a hard time sitting still for longer stretches—if one runs off after only one turn, that's OK. Just continue the game with the other twin as long as the players remaining are still having fun. If the first twin decides to come back, simply have him pick up where he left off. If no one wants to play anymore, no sweat—pack up the game and try again another day. Expecting 3-year-olds to sit perfectly still through an entire board game is unrealistic. Over time and with practice, you will see that your young twins will be able to sit for longer stretches, they will be more cooperative during the game, and the games will be more meaningful for them (ie, there is more to it than just moving a red game piece around in a random circle). If one twin wants to play a game with an older sibling, great! Encourage the twins to split up when they feel like it.

⫷ Preparing for Preschool

The idea of your young twins spending a couple of hours in a classroom setting away from their parents, siblings, and possibly each other can be quite a change for everyone involved. If your twins have spent time in a child care setting, the transition may not be as dramatic as for those who have been cared for at home or in a smaller group setting. Our generation may or may not have attended preschool back when we were young. Today, however, education experts agree that the experience of a preschool program can help kids learn more effectively when kindergarten comes along. We're talking about a fun, relaxed preschool atmosphere, and not any sort of rigorous academic curriculum! Three-year-olds usually participate 2 or 3 half days a week, while 4-year-olds can participate 3 or 4 half days a week.

Preschool registration happens at different times depending on where you live. In general for most areas, looking at preschool options a year before you plan on enrolling your twins is a good idea. Busy urban settings can be more competitive, and infants on preschool waiting lists are not uncommon in big cities.

In the months leading up to preschool, you'll want to provide your twins with some practice for the experience. Look around your community for options. Public libraries usually offer a story hour or craft sessions for each young age group. These story hours are a great way for your twins to practice sitting quietly in a group while listening to a story. The fact that these programs are usually free is a bonus. Your twins will learn some social etiquette by being in a room of 3-year-olds. Twins may be accustomed to close physical

Twin Tip!

Once upon a time, I took our twins, recently turned 3 years old, to a library story hour. After about 5 minutes, both boys started wandering around the room instead of sitting quietly to listen to the story. I gathered them together in the back of the room and quietly told them, just one time, "Let's try to sit and listen. If you can't sit and listen, we'll have to leave so we don't disturb the other kids." That day, the boys just weren't interested. I wanted them to appreciate these sorts of experiences and have positive associations with them—not to remember their mom nagging them for 30 minutes to hush and listen. So I simply gathered the boys up and we left. No sense in forcing the issue—this is supposed to be *fun* for the kids. Just try again another day. Keep exposing your twins to the idea of library story hour and similar experiences, and they'll learn to appreciate them.

contact with one another—but they'll need to learn that they can't be quite so cozy with others around them.

Another way to get your twins ready for preschool is to visit your area's public and school playgrounds after school hours. Get to know a variety of parks around your home to keep the trips interesting. Your twins will have fun on different types of equipment and feel quite comfortable at their preschool playground when the time comes. Your twins will also gain a little experience meeting and playing with other kids at the playground.

Look into your local park district youth offerings and recreational youth sports. Always ask if they offer a twin discount! Soccer is a great gender-neutral choice that boy-girl twins would enjoy. Park districts often offer a 3-year-old "class" specifically for a parent to drop the child off so that the child gets used to the idea of being on his own for a bit. To ease the transition, if your twins are in the same class, they can provide some comfort for each other when their parent leaves. At these types of classes, my twin boys were so excited to see new toys to play with that they didn't mind at all that Mom was leaving for a while. I had tears myself, though, the first couple of times, and didn't know if I felt better or worse that the boys weren't crying at these goodbyes. With a little practice getting out there with your twins, you'll all be ready to make the leap to 2 mornings a week of preschool quite smoothly.

Twin Tip!

When your twins attend preschool, they will bring home mountains of adorable craft projects and paintings. The artwork and drawings of 2 students can quickly accumulate and overwhelm a home. How can you preserve the highlights of your kids' projects while minimizing clutter? You can take digital photos of each child *individually* holding his or her artistic creation(s). You'll have documentation of the art and what your child looked like when she created the art, without taking up physical space on a shelf. Your twins will beam with pride when showing off their creation. After taking a digital picture, you can even hang the artwork in an art gallery on your twins' bedroom wall by using blue painter's tape. The tape can be rearranged multiple times without damaging painted walls or woodwork. An art gallery of preschool projects is a great way to boost your twins' self-esteem and encourage future projects! If the projects get crumpled or thrown out, no worries, because you've saved the projects with your digital camera!

Many parents of twins wonder if they should keep their twins in the same classroom for preschool, or separate them into 2 different classes. If your preschool is a small program, you may have no choice because all the 3-year-olds may be together in a single class. If there are 2 separate classrooms, you'll have to decide for your family on the best strategy.

For our family's situation, our decision for class placement was pretty straightforward. We felt that our identical twin sons looked so similar that the teachers and other students would be confused all year as to who each twin was. We didn't want our sons to hear the question, "Which one are you?" all year long. I wanted to de-emphasize the boys' "twinness" and give the boys a chance to show others who they are as a person, as an individual. I also felt that 2 mornings a week of being in 2 separate classrooms wouldn't be that big of a deal, considering the boys are together the other 5 days a week, 24 hours a day. In addition, I felt that after some practice with separate preschool classrooms, the transition into separate classrooms in the higher grades should be a little easier.

Twin Tip!

If your twins are in 2 classrooms in school, prepare in advance for special school days such as Meet the Teacher Day. Arrange for both parents to attend, or have Grandma or another trusted adult help on the special day. Let the teachers know your situation in advance and that you plan on spending time in both classrooms to see both kids and both environments. If only one parent can attend, explain the situation to the teachers so they can fill you in on important information that you may have missed while moving between the 2 classes.

The issue of twin placement in classrooms is currently a very hot issue as many families feel that their kids would do better in school if their twins were in the same class. These families argue that the family, not the school, should make the final decision of class placement. New legislation has been popping up in various states giving families the final say in whether twins are placed together or separately. Each family must assess its own situation and decide what will work best for it. Some families find that keeping twins together in the early years helps smooth the way for eventual separation in the higher grades.

Twin Tip!

Parents can observe the classroom dynamic, meet class-mates, get to know the teacher better, make their child feel special, and help out the school all in the matter of a couple of hours by volunteering in their children's classroom(s). Preschools usually love parents' hands-on involvement in the classroom, and kids get a real ego-boost to show off their class and parent to each other! My kids' school experiences were somewhat of a mystery to me until I spent some time assisting in the classroom. After you spend a little time with the class, you'll be able to ask each child specific questions about friends or workstations because you've seen the class in action firsthand. Even if you work outside the home, I recommend arranging for a morning off from work to spend an hour or two with the class. If your twins are in 2 separate classrooms, be sure to post your volunteer dates prominently on the family cal-endar, and talk about the timing with the kids to prevent any jealousy or concerns about fairness.

ᕲ One-on-one Time—It's Still Important

Continue to carve out as much one-on-one time as you can with each of your twins during their preschool years. Recognizing and stealing moments for special time throughout a regular day is a good strategy—read with one twin while the other is playing with air-planes, for example. Continue to take just one twin alone on outings with you when another parent or adult can help out.

We've taken one-on-one time to a new level in our family with special airplane trips with Mom—we have extended family scattered around the country and have found airfare for 2 much more afford-able than for the whole family of 6. We can reduce traveling costs, visit faraway family, and squeeze in special time with each child, all at once! We rotate these trips through the birth order to be fair to all 4 of our kids. These special trips are such a treat for our kids, and I always come away from each experience with a new appreciation for who each of my children are as individuals.

⁊ Two Distinct Individuals, Now More Than Ever

Whenever I meet someone who happened to grow up as a twin, I always ask if there was anything he would have preferred his parents to have done differently. Most of the time the response I hear is some variation on a similar theme: I wish our parents didn't…"give us the same thing for our birthday," "dress us in identical outfits," "expect us to share everything."

While some people assume all twins are the same, others take it to the other extreme. Many people ask me if my twin sons are opposites—is one social while the other is a recluse? Is one more talkative and the other quiet? Or, my favorite, "Which is the good one?" These questions imply that each twin's character traits are defined as the opposite of those of his twin brother. Of course this is not the case—they are individuals, and each child is complete on his own.

Any individual can be similar to another in some respects and different in other ways. Everybody, whether born as a twin or not, desires to be treated as an individual. Parents of all twins, identical or same-sex twins more so, need to think about this on a daily basis. You're a busy parent and it may be quicker or more efficient at

Twin Tip!

When you are busy parenting young twins, try not to get caught up in the day-to-day craziness and lose sight of the big picture. Take a moment to step back from time to time to evaluate your twins' experiences. How will they remember their childhood? Treat each of the twins as an individual. When you take pictures, for example, make sure you aren't always pairing the twins together for the camera. Your twins will thank you for your efforts when they are adults!

times to treat your twins as a unit, but I encourage you to treat your twins as 2 children who happen to have been born on the same day.

A great way to treat your twins as individuals is to read their bedtime stories to them individually at night. When our twin boys were babies and toddlers, we were operating in survival mode, so we usually read to them simultaneously. As the years progressed and our twins were easier to care for, we saw that it would benefit both boys to have their bedtime stories read to them one-on-one. Reading to each twin separately boosts early reading skills and creates a calmer atmosphere in which to quiet down and settle in with a good book. The time and work to read to your twins individually is well worth the effort. The twins don't distract each other and they get a lot more out of the experience. Try to alternate which twin reads with which parent each night. Be realistic, though, and on late nights or if one parent is handling bedtime solo, gather everyone to snuggle up for the bedtime stories.

Twins know how to share well, having shared their parents with each other since they were newborns, but expecting twins to share *all* their things *all* the time is unrealistic. You'll want to have a system to give each child her own personal space. Even if your twins share

Twin Tip!

My identical twins didn't quite realize that they were different from most other kids until their preschool years. All of a sudden they realized that not everyone else has an identical-looking brother the same age! Whenever someone would ask one of my twins, "Which one are you?" he would look at them with bemused disbelief. If your twins are the same sex, dress them in different clothing to help friends and classmates know who is who. If your twins look a great deal alike, *talk* about it with your twins. Your twins are so used to life with a twin that they may not realize that others can't tell them apart! You can even role-play social situations—teach your twins to introduce themselves clearly, and teach each child how to politely correct someone who has guessed his identity incorrectly.

a bedroom, you can provide each twin with a distinctly colored box that they can keep their special things in—a rock collection, a favor from a friend's party, whatever they decide is important to them.

Remind each twin to respect their siblings' personal space—older and younger siblings' space as well, as twins can outnumber an older brother and confiscate a special toy by sheer manpower alone. Give each twin her own distinct-looking piggy bank to collect loose coins. Institute a house rule that you can only check your own piggy bank's contents!

In your living and play areas, create separate play stations so that there are interesting things to do at different places in the home—one twin can play Lincoln Logs in one area while the other goes in the other room to listen to a kids' CD player. Don't expect your twins to play with the same items all the time. Give each child some space and breathing room, and your days will be more harmonious.

On birthdays and holidays, give each child distinctive presents. At 3 and 4 years of age, each child has particular interests—pick up on these differences and use them as inspiration for giving separate gifts. Adult twins groan when they remember all the times that they received 2 of the same item, maybe in different colors. When our twins were 3 years old, we noticed that sharks fascinated Ryan and Andrew was interested in fire trucks, so on their birthday we ran with these themes. The shark-themed books and toys lived on as Ryan's, and Andrew's new fire truck was Andrew's. Emphasize to gift-giving family members to look for distinctive gifts for your twins—they'll likely appreciate a little coaching.

All toys that enter your home will eventually get shared exten-sively—after all, playing with *all* the cumulative toys, rather than just your own portion, is more fun! But initially, on gift-giving occa-sions, give each child at least a day or two with his new toy before he is expected to share with others. After the first couple of days or a period that seems appropriate, the new items can become part of the public domain, fair game for all.

If your twins are squabbling over who gets to play with a new item, use the egg timer trick. Give each child a timed turn with the toy, and rotate turns. The egg timer helps reassure your twins that the turns will be fair.

Another way to emphasize each twin's individuality is to assign a signature color to each child. At the preschool age kids usually have preferred colors—use these colors for clothes, coats, toothbrushes, and backpacks to clearly indicate who the owner is and streamline the process of getting ready each day. The more distinct the twins' personal items are, the less confusion as to whose coat is whose will occur. Ah, family harmony.

Twin Tip!

In the preschool years, your twins' social circles will expand. Is one of your twin's classmates having a birthday party? Take just the one invited twin to the party and leave the other twin with a trusted caregiver. These parties are a wonderful way for each of your twins to gain social skills independently. Are you worried that the other twin will be sad? There will be plenty of opportunities over the years for these situations to even out. As a parent, lead by example—be cheerful and assure the other twin that soon it will be her turn to go to a party while the other twin stays home. Your child probably won't even know to be sad if you do a good job of discussing the situation in a positive light!

🐾 Consistency and Discipline

By the time your twins are 3 and 4 years old, they should have a clear understanding of what your house rules are and a sense of what is appropriate behavior. Hopefully you've been able to lay down a consistent framework of rules in the twins' toddler years on which you can continue to build. High expectations of your twins' behavior from an early age has lots of benefits—instead of having to undo a year's worth of poor behavior, you are providing positive reinforcement for appropriate behavior.

Three- and 4-year-olds, while more mature than toddlers, are still growing and learning, and will continue to test limits and rules. The testing of limits is age-appropriate behavior and not a deliberate attempt on your twins' part to drive you insane! Your kids will test you in different situations to see if the rules still hold water. Your twins are also meeting new friends at school and recreation programs who behave in different ways, and they will wonder if they can try out some of those new behaviors at home with you. As parents, you need to hold strong and stick to the house rules.

If your child disobeys a rule, don't just give endless warnings with no consequences—give a *time-out*. Remember that a proper time-out takes place in a boring location for 1 minute per one year of the child's age (ie, 3 or 4 minutes for preschoolers). When time is up, tell your child in 1 or 2 sentences what she did wrong, have her apologize to the appropriate person if the situation calls for it, and move on with your day. Don't dwell on the misbehavior or give it undue attention—you don't want to reward poor behavior with extra attention!

Twin Tip!

Your twins are smart. As an example, let's say one of your twins throws a bouncy ball in the kitchen. You warn your child, "No balls in the kitchen. Take that out of here or Dad will take the ball." If the other twin heard this conversation and then proceeds to throw her own ball in the kitchen, you should follow up with taking the ball away, even if it was the second twin who misbehaved. Why? You do not need to give each of your twins separate warnings about the same issue when they are both present for the original warning! Let your twins know, "When I say something to one of you, I am saying it to both of you!" If you use this consistent pattern to deal with twins' misbehavior, you'll save a lot of time and energy down the line by preventing your twins from experimenting to find different parental responses.

Balancing the Family Dynamic

You may notice a new phenomenon in your home now that your twins are preschool aged—teaming up against other siblings or friends. By this age your twins have a tight bond with each other and consider each other teammates of sorts. Be aware that your twins may, perhaps unwittingly, gang up on others. Nip this sort of behavior in the bud. Explain to your twins that you expect them to be kind to and share with *all* of their siblings, not just with their twin.

Preschool-aged twins may preferentially share things with each other, but instantly become territorial if their older brother or younger sister shows interest—the tight twin bond illustrating itself once again. Monitor these situations to make sure the single-born siblings aren't getting railroaded or just passively allowing certain situations to keep the peace. This is a form of bullying and it shouldn't be tolerated.

Don't forget, as discussed in "Kind But Effective Discipline" in Chapter 6, that you should never ask, "Who started it?" A fight takes 2 kids and if you ask, "Who started it?" your twins will learn to manipulate your reactions. You want them to learn how to settle their differences on their own, without an ever-present parent mediator—not to learn how to pin the blame on the other guy.

Expectations on Outings

As your twins grow older, you're probably going on more family outings to area museums, zoos, and the like. New situations run more smoothly if you remind your twins what you expect of their behavior *beforehand*. When you get to the zoo, before everyone unbuckles to get out of the car, take a moment to talk with the kids about what you expect. Remind them, "The zoo can be a busy place and there are lots of cool things to see, but everyone has to *stay together as a group*. Don't just run off if you see the giraffe! Tell Dad you want to see the giraffes and we'll all go together." Exercise good crowd control by reminding your twins beforehand, when everything is calm, before any such moment occurs. Your twins will be reminded to use their self-control and you won't lose them in a crowd of strangers. Give your twins lots of practice and they'll learn with repeated outings.

Anticipatory talks before new situations can help the kids remember how to behave—these talks are a kind and gentle way to lay out expectations that you can draw upon if someone behaves poorly. If you're all going to have to wait in line at the post office, remind your twins beforehand that you expect them to stand quietly with you and not run around loudly. If you are going to a friend's house for lunch, remind everyone of proper behavior before you get out of the car.

When my 4 kids were quite young, I took them to museums and zoos by myself numerous times. I suppose I wasn't truly by myself—I had my 4 kids with me! We've had some great adventures, the kids have learned a lot, and the trips have boosted my confidence as a parent. I always received comments from other parents, though, who were apparently shocked that my kids weren't running away from me. I've heard, "I don't know how you do it alone; I couldn't because my kid's a runner," many times. How can you keep your kids together as a group on an outing? Even before getting out of the car, remind everyone of the rule of staying as a group. Then, during the outing, if one of your kids does run off too far, she should temporarily lose the privilege of walking independently "like a big kid." She should hold your hand or hold onto the stroller (if you're using one for a younger sibling) for the next 10 minutes, and if she is well behaved, she can earn back the privilege of walking independently, like a big kid, *with the group*. If one or more of the kids are not getting the message and are repeatedly running off, you'll have to cut the outing short, explaining to your kid(s) that because they can't follow the rules, they cannot stay and have fun. Cutting a zoo trip short if someone's misbehaving is not pleasant, but letting your kids know that behaving properly and staying with the group is more important.

When Twins Collide

Twins are extremely close, yet when twins fight, look out! Twins' fights can be more extreme and emotional than fights between other siblings precisely because they are so close—feelings are hurt more deeply when a stronger connection exists.

How can you reduce the amount of infighting between your twins? Look for frequent trouble spots and figure out solutions. In our family, car seat location was quite a hot topic. After a particularly bad week filled with fights over who got to sit in which car seat, I had to lay down the law. We would alternate between 2 car seats on a monthly basis—Andrew sat in the preferred seat during September, for example, and Ryan would sit in that seat during October, and so on. Everyone knew what to expect, and our kids knew their parents wouldn't waffle, so they didn't bother trying to change the system. The bonus of this system is that your kids learn the months of the year. Perhaps your twins both desire the same chair at the dinner table—if your twins are having repeated arguments over the same issue, strategize to see if a new system can promote peace.

Advanced Toilet Training and Independence

Do not despair if your twins are not fully toilet trained by their third birthday. Continue to be as patient and supportive as you can be, which is easier said than done. Toileting accidents can be extremely frustrating, more so if your kids have been training for a while. After the third birthday, toilet training can take on a new dimension—a 3-year-old can be more stubborn than a 2-year-old and is more likely to dig in his heels if there is a battle of the wills.

Power struggles can be more frequent and severe than in the past—as a parent, you need to relax as best you can, as frustrating as the situation may be. If you get more emotional and upset with your twins, they may resist toileting even more, in a vicious cycle, as a result. At the preschool age a child truly has a mind of her own and ultimately, she has to decide for herself to toilet on her own.

If you have a difficult week filled with accidents, you may have to back off for a while. Make sure your twins help clean up their

Twin Tip!

Sometimes one twin may backtrack and start having toileting accidents, and as a result get more attention for cleanup and lectures. Be careful of paying one twin too much attention for accidents—his twin may start to also have accidents in a subconscious attempt to get some more attention.

accidents and have them get their own fresh clothes from the drawer to help them realize how much easier it is to pee and poop into the toilet, not in one's underwear!

Use success sticker reward charts in the case of toileting regression. You can make the charts as specific as you like—if only one twin is having poop accidents, for example, create just one poop chart for her to help her get back on track.

True toilet training is complete when your twins do not need reminders to use the toilet. When you notice that they've been doing well with parental reminders, back off a bit and see if they remind themselves. The sooner your twins learn to remind themselves to use the toilet, the more independent they will be. If you require further assitance with toilet training, or your twins are having problems such as constipation, consult with your pediatrician.

ꙮ Emotional and Social Support for Parents

Your day-to-day routine with your twins is much easier than in the past, but it's still a lot of work. Parents of young twins need to seek out ways to relieve the stress and laugh about the current craziness of their lives. A positive mental attitude will go a long way in helping you survive the chaos of each day. Spilt milk? Kids not listening the fifth time you've told them something? The next time you feel yourself losing your temper, try to see the humor in the situation.

Is there splashed bathwater all over the bathroom floor? Have your crew grab towels with you and mop it up, telling them, "Well, this is one way to get the floor clean!" There are a lot of mishaps that can occur each day—life will be more fun if you can laugh about it and move on.

Parenthood can be a tough road—having comrades with you helps. Now that your twins are participating in more activities and attending preschool, you have a lot more opportunities to meet other parents of similar-aged kids. Reach out to meet new acquaintances— it is very therapeutic to share war stories and see that some of the struggles in your home are happening in other homes too! You're not alone—parents share many of the same issues, whether or not they have twins. You can laugh about the struggles and move on,

Twin Tip!

Some days you may feel like you're telling your preschool twins the same things 100 times! Use humor so that you don't lose your cool. Your twins learn how to handle tense situations by watching you. When one of my then-4-year-old twins was not listening to me one evening, I wondered aloud, "Can we buy Andrew some new ears at the Ear Store? I think his are broken—he's not listening to his mom!" Andrew knew I was being goofy (not sarcastic—there's a big difference) and amidst the giggling, he understood that I was trying to get his attention. I had made my point in a fun way, not in a nagging, unpleasant way. And once I got him laughing, lo and behold, he was a lot more receptive to what I was saying.

remembering that each phase will pass quickly. If you're a naturally shy person, practice making small talk with other parents at a public park. Even if small talk doesn't lead to a lifelong friendship, it boosts your mood and takes you out of your own little world.

When out around town running errands, our family saw that the comments from strangers about our twins did not slow down. If anything, having a fourth child close in age increased the amount of

Twin Tip!

As your twins grow older, keep trying your best to attend your local twin club meetings, even if you only attend once in a while. You may feel that you've outgrown these meetings because you've moved past the newborn stage, but if you can give another new parent of twins some baby advice that you've lived and learned, you can see how far you've come on your parenting journey now that your twins are older. That can be quite a confidence builder, which can keep your spirits up.

comments we received! Far and away the most common comment is, "You've sure got your hands full!" Sometimes this line is delivered in a pitying tone with some head shaking, as if to say, "Wow, poor you!" Don't let these comments get under your skin. I am so used to hearing this phrase by now that I am ready with my reply: "They're very good kids, and we're so lucky."

View the interactions with interested strangers from your children's point of view. What should my twin sons think when we go out in public and people seem to feel sorry for their mom because of *them?* I never want my twins to feel that they are a burden on me. Even though I am talking to the stranger and not my kids, I want to send the message to my twins *everyday* that they are loved, wanted, and wonderful.

Twin Tip!

I find that interactions with inquisitive, curious strangers can be a helpful way to boost my twins' self-esteem by complimenting them to others. An overheard compliment can be a lot more effective than simply telling your kids directly, "You are good kids and I love you."

❧ Budgeting and Practical Matters

Parenthood can be expensive even with just one child. Twins seem to need many of the same things at the same time, and therefore can seem much more costly. When you're providing toys and experiences for your twins, remember that cost does not determine quality. Preschool children can have a grand time with an empty cardboard box—it can be whatever you imagine it to be and can change on a whim. The box can be a spaceship, train, house, or whatever your twins are in the mood for! The less a toy does, the more the kids think.

"Grocery store" and "restaurant" are 2 of our all-time favorite games to play. Save empty real food containers like butter tubs and cake mix boxes, clean them out, and use them as your groceries. You don't even need an actual toy play kitchen—you can create one out of an empty box by drawing a range on top with markers and decorating it however you please.

> ## *Twin Tip!*
>
> Don't blow the bank buying toys for your twins. Think outside the box for interesting playthings. I found tailor's measuring tape at a craft store for a dollar, and my kids could spend an afternoon measuring everything around the house. In fact, the first time I heard my son Ryan count to 50 was when he was measuring my bathroom countertop with the measuring tape. Some of the best toys don't even have to be toys at all!

The public library can be a parent of twins' best friend for sticking with a budget. Make a point to visit the library as much as you can to treat your twins. Let each child pick out his own book or two to give them a sense of ownership over the book. Having plenty of books available in your home will encourage your twins to become lifelong readers.

> ## *Twin Tip!*
>
> Another bonus to museum and zoo memberships is that it is easier to plan spontaneous outings. Busy parents of twins don't have lots of extra time to research and explore countless different options for a day trip. With a museum or zoo membership, you can take your family out without having to think or plan too hard! Once you've made a museum trip a couple of times, you'll really get to know the lay of the land. Bring your lunch along and you've got quite an affordable family day.

Budgeting for a family vacation is difficult when your family has 4 or more people. Airfare can be quite steep, especially because airlines charge kids older than 2 years the same fares as adults. You can take more vacation in your local area by considering family memberships to your area zoos and museums. Memberships are quite cost-effective for larger families and often pay for themselves in fewer than 2 visits in a year! When you use a family membership, you don't feel pressured to see all the exhibits in one day. If one of the kids is cranky, you can leave early. We like having zoo and aquarium memberships so that when the weather is nice, we can go to the zoo, and during hot or snowy seasons, we can go to the indoor aquarium.

Twin Tip!

When you take your preschooler twins on outings, keep a stash of sandwich-sized plastic bags with your supplies. Distribute a healthy snack during the outing by handing out individual bags to each child—a more cost-effective method than purchasing convenience-sized packages at the store.

Another way to have some affordable family bonding time is with family movie picnics. Spread out some blankets in your family room, pop some popcorn, and put in an age-appropriate DVD. Let the cuddling and bonding commence! These picnics cost hardly anything, but can be so much fun for all of you.

Enjoying the Here and Now

Savor playtime with your preschooler twins. Enjoy the fruits of your labor over the last 4 years. You've put in so much effort and energy into your twins, and now you can stand back and enjoy these wonderful people that you have nurtured and guided. Don't be in a rush for the next stage of life. Play an extra game of Uno or Candy Land with your twins and enjoy this magical stage of their lives.

CHAPTER 8

The Early Years End— As Your Twins Grow

Our twin sons adore their big brother, and as preschoolers, they loved to accompany him to his bus stop on school mornings. One morning was garbage and recycling pickup day. After the big kids' bus zoomed away to school, we returned to our home with 2 large, now empty bins sitting at the end of the driveway. Without hesitation, Ryan and Andrew each grabbed one of the wheeled containers and began to roll the behemoths back into our garage. The bins towered well over their heads, and I called out, "That's OK, guys, I can get those!"

They quickly replied, "Mom, we're strong; we can do it!" Each bin was returned to its usual place in the garage, and I praised and thanked each boy, thinking, "Wow, this is the life!" After years of tending to my *twins'* every need, the boys were now turning the tables and pitching in with our *family's* needs!

ಎ The Journey

Time flies when you are having fun! In the blink of an eye, your twins will grow from highly dependent babies into walking, talking, imaginative little people! Raising twins through their early years is quite an endeavor. Parents of twins learn so much through the process—we learn just as much about ourselves as we learn about our children. Did you know that you have an unlimited capacity for patience and love? You can handle feeding 2 babies around the clock. You can change endless diapers. You can resolve the conflicts of warring toddler twins, and teach rambunctious twins sharing a bedroom to stay in their big-kid beds.

Give yourself credit for being capable and strong! You will succeed in parenting your twins during the challenging early years! In the beginning, parents of multiples may feel shocked and overwhelmed when they discover that they will have more than one baby—but any anxiety felt in the past is replaced with confident efficiency.

Your twin parenting skills adapt through the years as your twins grow. In the early days, parents of twins keep a synchronized schedule of feeding and constant care. As your twins grow older, your job as a parent shifts to managing the psychologic aspects of raising 2 loving yet independent people. As your twins grow through the coming years, you will be focusing more on nurturing each twin as an individual.

Continue to raise your twins with confidence! You will help your twins through many milestones and transitions in their early years. You are now an organizational expert—use your impressive skills to streamline your family's needs in the coming years so that you all have more time for fun. Enjoy watching the fruits of your labor unfold!

Built-in Life Lessons

Built-in life lessons are the beauty of raising multiple children close in age. Twins learn *patience,* as their parents have more than one child for whom to care. Twins learn how to *share.* They have been sharing their mom and dad from the beginning, and as they grow their sharing skills get lots of practice each day as they always have other playmates nearby. Twins learn *empathy.* Being so close to their siblings, they truly develop an understanding of other people's point of view. Many experts believe that school-aged twins can be more socially savvy than their single-born peers because they have continual practice negotiating and interacting with others.

Two Unique Individuals— A Special Bond

The twin bond is beautiful and will always be special for your children and family. However, as your twins grow, continue to give your kids plenty of opportunities to be individuals and pursue their own interests. They will have different strengths, and these traits should be celebrated. Twins will always have a strong relationship, but each individual twin will go on to make his own friends, participate in different sports and activities, and have different life experiences.

Make sure you continue to provide each of your twins with a separate birthday cake each year! Do your best to help each of your twins find ways of establishing her own individuality, separate from her siblings. Encourage your family members to respect each twin's individuality to help each of your children navigate their social worlds with a better sense of self-identity.

🐦 An Eye Toward the Future

What does the future hold for your family? Among other fun surprises sure to come your way, your twins will one day be eligible for learner's permits for a (gasp!) *driver's license!* Many parents of older twins have joked with me, "It gets easier all the time, but just wait until they're driving!" How will we handle the transition to the teenage driving years? We parents of twins will navigate this and other hurdles the same way we've adjusted to so many other milestones— one day at a time!

Facts Every Parent of Twins Should Know

*T*wins are identical or fraternal. *Identical* (monozygotic) twins result from a single fertilized egg that has divided into 2, giving each twin identical genetic material. *Fraternal* (dizygotic) twins result from 2 separate eggs being fertilized by 2 separate sperm, giving each twin different genetic material.

Identical twins consistently occur at about 1% of all births around the world. Identical twinning appears to be unrelated to family history, maternal age, or any ethnic, geographic, or socioeconomic patterns, and has so far eluded explanation as to its occurrence.

Fraternal twins, on the other hand, have varying percentages of occurrence in different populations and places in the world. Fraternal twins are associated with a family history of twinning, advanced maternal age, and the use of fertility treatments. A family history of twins affects the maternal lineage, meaning that the tendency to produce twins is carried only by the mother, not the father. A twinning family history is a tendency of mothers to ovulate more than one egg at a time in a single monthly cycle. Twins do not, as a rule, skip a generation because these ovulatory events are random each month.

❧ The Distinction Between Identical and Fraternal Twins

Because fraternal, or dizygotic, twins are 2 separate fertilized eggs, they usually develop 2 separate amniotic sacs, placentas, and supporting structures. Identical, or monozygotic, twins may or may not share the same amniotic sac, depending on how early the single fertilized egg divides into 2.

If twins are a boy and a girl, clearly they are fraternal twins, as they do not have the same DNA. A boy has XY chromosomes and a girl has XX chromosomes. Girl-boy twins occur when one X egg is fertilized with an X sperm, and a Y sperm fertilizes the other X egg.

Sometimes health care professionals identify same-sex twins as fraternal or identical based on ultrasound findings or by examining the membranes at the time of delivery. The best way to determine if twins are identical or fraternal is by examining each child's DNA. Occasionally a family is told that their twins are fraternal based on placenta findings, when they are in fact identical. Other times, a family may see the minor differences in identical twins and declare the twins fraternal based on these differences in appearance. There are a few commercial laboratories that, for a fee, will send families DNA collection kits to determine if the twins are identical or fraternal. The families swab the insides of each child's cheek for a DNA sample and send the kit back to the laboratory to await results.

Identical twins have the same DNA; however, they may not look exactly identical to one another because of environmental factors such as womb position and life experiences after being born. Our family joke about one of our twin's stitches for a lacerated upper lip was that he wanted to distinguish himself from his identical twin brother! In addition to life's bumps, bruises, and differing hairstyles, a child's DNA is constantly adapting to that child's experiences. Different stretches of one's DNA can turn on or off in response to environmental surroundings—therefore, over time, a pair of identical twins' DNA becomes more and more distinctive. All twins, whether fraternal or identical, are truly 2 separate, unique individuals.

⚘ More and More Twins!

In 2009 the Centers for Disease Control and Prevention National Center for Health Statistics published 2006 data on US births according to a wide variety of characteristics. The twin birth rate in 2006 was 3.2%. The twin birth rate has increased steadily through the years—it has increased 42% since 1990 and 70% since 1980. National Vital Statistics Reports found that the most important trends leading to the rise in multiple births are maternal age and the use of fertility treatments. Older women have a higher chance of ovulating 2 eggs during a single monthly cycle. In addition, women who undergo fertility treatments or hormone therapy to induce ovulation are more likely to ovulate multiple eggs. In vitro fertilization techniques of implanting more than one fertilized egg at a time have been quite successful—so successful, in fact, that in recent years there has been a transition toward implanting fewer fertilized eggs in mothers to reduce the complications of multiple pregnancy and preterm birth.

Where do the most twin births occur in the United States? Interestingly, the National Center for Health Statistics report showed that for the years 2003 to 2006, twins accounted for more than 4% of all births in Connecticut, Massachusetts, and New Jersey.

If Your Twins Are Born Early

*T*he majority of twins do well after delivery. However, multiples have a greater chance of premature delivery compared with single-born babies. This appendix serves as an overview of issues that preterm babies might face, and will explain some terms and therapies that a family may encounter in the neonatal intensive care unit (NICU). If you are pregnant with twins, do your best to keep a positive spirit and healthy outlook on your pregnancy—but do familiarize yourself with some of the following issues to prepare in case your family has an early delivery.

A full-term pregnancy is 37 weeks long or more, yet twin pregnancies usually deliver, on average, around 36 weeks. The National Vital Statistics Reports show that 60% of twins born in 2005 arrived prior to 37 weeks' gestation. The final weeks of pregnancy are a time for growing babies' weight gain and lung maturation. For this reason, if your twins are born early, they may face low birth weight and respiratory issues.

Some twins who are born a little early may need time in the NICU to gain weight before going home. Other babies may have respiratory issues in addition to a need to gain weight. More significantly preterm twins may have additional issues. Each newborn will be evaluated and treated as an individual, and twins may have disparate needs at birth. Preterm delivery can be scary for parents and families, but the good news is that modern medicine has made wonderful advancements toward care for premature babies.

Nutrition

If you are physically able, you can start pumping breast milk soon after delivery—breast milk is the perfect nutrition for small or preterm babies. Pumping will help boost your milk supply. If your babies cannot tolerate feeding by mouth yet, the milk can be frozen and fed at a later date. A high-quality, hospital-grade breast pump can help you double pump breast milk quickly and easily. Recruit your nurses and the hospital lactation consultants for assistance and advice.

Breast milk is ideal, but there are also formulas specially made for babies born before 36 weeks. Maximizing the babies' nutritional intake is a key step toward weight gain. In addition, supplemental iron will help boost premature babies' blood supply.

Babies who cannot yet suck and swallow from a bottle may require nasogastric tube feeds, in which breast milk or formula is fed via a small tube entered in the nose that goes to the stomach. Tube feeding helps the stomach and intestines stay healthy and accustomed to digesting milk until the baby develops her own suck reflex to feed.

ᕫᕽ Respiratory Issues

During the final weeks in the womb, the lungs form a substance called *surfactant,* which helps the lungs develop elasticity, like a balloon, to open up and take air after delivery. Babies born early may lack this substance and may develop respiratory distress syndrome (RDS) as a result. Corticosteroids such as betamethasone are usually given to a mother in preterm labor before 34 weeks to help prevent RDS. If a baby has signs of severe RDS, surfactant treatment is given to the baby soon after delivery and in the first couple of days of life, and the baby will require the help of a breathing tube and ventilator. Babies with less severe RDS may require a nasal tube with oxygen. Preterm babies who require oxygen for longer periods may go on to develop chronic lung disease.

Preterm babies commonly have apnea of prematurity, which means they have episodes when they forget to breathe, requiring stimulation to continue breathing. Stimulant medication can help control apnea of prematurity, which usually resolves by the time the baby is 40 weeks' post-conceptional age.

ᕫᕽ Jaundice

Jaundice is a yellowing of newborn babies' skin and eyes. It happens when a chemical called bilirubin builds up in the baby's blood. Bilirubin is a byproduct of old red blood cells, and is removed by the liver. Most newborns, even if healthy and full term, have some degree of increased bilirubin because the immature red blood cells of a newborn break down more quickly. In addition, the liver is immature and not fully handling the extra bilirubin.

A simple laboratory test measures the amount of bilirubin in the blood to evaluate the degree of jaundice. Pediatricians are concerned about jaundice because high levels of bilirubin, if left untreated, can cause deafness or brain damage. Light phototherapy can reduce the bilirubin levels if needed. A baby receiving phototherapy looks like a baby visiting a tanning salon; skin exposure helps the treatment be more effective, and the baby will even wear mini-sunglasses to protect his eyes.

ஒ Other Concerns

- Low birth weight or premature babies who need help maintaining their body temperature are placed in radiant warmer beds or Isolettes (incubators).
- Infections are a concern for preterm babies with an immature immune system.
- Babies born extremely early will require eye examinations to screen for retinal problems, as well as head ultrasounds to evaluate for any bleeding from fragile blood vessels.
- Some babies have patent ductus arteriosus (PDA), in which a normal fetal connection within the major heart vessels does not close after delivery the way it should. A PDA can be treated with medication; if the medication fails to close the connection, surgery may be required.

ஒ Bonding in the Neonatal Intensive Care Unit

Give your babies names as soon as possible. Naming your babies will help your family and hospital staff bond with the babies. Get to know the NICU staff; they are knowledgeable and will become part of your extended family. Bring in family photos and special mementos for each of your babies' bedsides.

Initially, it may not be safe for parents to hold a premature baby. When the babies are medically stabilized, you will be able to hold your babies and participate in *kangaroo care*. Kangaroo care, direct skin-to-skin contact with your baby, is great for moms *and* dads, and is as beneficial for parents as it is for the babies. Parent-child bonding thrives on the sense of touch.

As your babies grow over time, you will be able to become more involved in their day-to-day care. You'll learn when your babies' care times are, and you can help take temperatures, change diapers, reposition the babies, and even give baths. Continue pumping breast milk and nurse your babies one at a time if you are able.

⫷ Going Home—When Is the Right Time?

It is possible that one of your twins may be able to come home before the other. Babies who are ready to go home from the hospital should be able to regulate their body temperature, take all their feedings by mouth, be gaining weight in a steady pattern, and have a home plan for any ongoing medical issues.

Your babies may need breathing and heart rate monitoring at home. Hospital staff will train you to learn how to use any necessary equipment. If one baby is able to come home before the other, use the opportunity to get into a routine before the other baby comes home. When both babies are home, coordinate feedings and nap times to occur at the same times each day.

⫷ Other Homecoming Concerns

If your twins were born before 35 weeks' gestation, needed oxygen at birth, or are still on oxygen, ask your pediatrician about monthly injections to prevent respiratory syncytial virus (RSV). In older kids or adults, RSV presents itself similar to a bad cold. However, babies born prematurely or who have chronic lung disease can develop a serious lung infection if they catch RSV. In addition, ask your twins' NICU staff about developmental clinic follow-ups to monitor your babies' developmental growth after being discharged home from the hospital.

The Triplet Parenting Experience—Advice That All Parents Can Use

Our twin sons are 18 months younger than our first son, so when our family goes out and about, strangers often ask us if our sons are triplets. Even though I had 4 kids within 4 years, my kids were born on 3 different birthdays, which made life a lot easier during their infancy stages! I have so much respect and admiration for families with triplets and more, and the unique challenges that they face in the early years. All families with multiples can benefit from the lessons that families with triplets have learned to stream-line care for their infants and keep their family organized.

To prepare this special section about triplets, I spoke with many wonderful families with triplets or quadruplets. Each of these families has beautiful multiples, and in many cases single-born children as well, yet each of these families has different structures and family schedules. Some moms work full time, some moms stopped work-ing outside the home to care for their children, and some moms are back at school to further their education. Despite dissimilar family structures, these families' successes have some consistent themes. Good organization is critical to survival, and multiples come with built-in benefits!

ᘍ Pregnancy Preparation

Just as with twins, parents of triplets need to be prepared for an early delivery. Mothers carrying triplets should expect to go on some form of bed rest around the 20-week point of the pregnancy. Bed rest may be at home initially with modified activities, and then advance to full hospitalized bed rest. Mothers of triplets need to eat considerably more calories to help their babies grow. Some moms find protein shakes are a healthy and convenient way to obtain extra calories.

Even during the pregnancy stages, parents of multiples can reach out to area Moms of Multiples groups as well as Internet support groups. Reaching out to other families with triplets can provide practical survival tips as well as reduce feelings of isolation. There are wonderful Internet support groups for families dealing with

> ## *Triplet Tip!*
>
> When you are pregnant with triplets, quadruplets, or more, you need to eat more calories than you would for a singleton or twin pregnancy. Consult with your obstetrician to ensure that you are meeting your caloric and protein intake needs.

various stages of triplets' lives, from pregnancy on through the teenage years.

While you are pregnant with your multiples, begin to research various options to recruit volunteers to assist your family during the challenging early months. Ask family, friends, neighbors, and your place of worship for support.

⅋ Synchronized Schedules

The great majority of triplet families stay sane their first exciting year by coordinating their babies' feeding and nap schedules. Families that start out feeding babies on a more casual as-needed basis quickly find themselves overwhelmed and adjust to streamline the process.

> ## *Triplet Tip!*
>
> Get your babies on a schedule and keep it. Your babies will need to drink milk every 3 to 4 hours. Feed 2 babies simultaneously and then feed the third baby.

Often when babies are sent home from the neonatal intensive care unit (NICU), they have a consistent feeding schedule, such as every 3 hours. Many triplet families take advantage of the existing NICU schedule and keep their babies on the same pattern, tweaking the 3 babies' schedules to work together more efficiently.

In the early weeks and months, many families obtain outside help with frequent feedings. With a second adult's assistance, infant triplets can feed at the same time—1 adult can feed 2 babies simultaneously while a second adult feeds the third. Alternatively, when a parent handles the 3 babies solo, 2 babies are fed simultaneously followed by the third. Nursing moms can nurse 2 of the babies together, and then feed the third baby a bottle of pumped breast milk.

ॐ Surviving the Early Months

Families have different strategies for handling the challenging weeks when they first bring their triplets home. Volunteers can help immensely in the daytime and nighttime. Ask your helpers to perform specific duties. They can feed the babies, do laundry, cook or bring along a meal, clean the house, or just hold the babies.

Many families arrange to have help with the first month of overnight feedings. One family that I spoke with had help from relatives—the grandmother arrived at the home each evening to handle overnight feeds for the first month the triplets were home; she would leave in the morning to refresh, and return again the following evening.

Triplet Tip!

One smart family with quadruplets used a great plan for nighttime feeds when their babies were infants. Mom and Dad would feed the babies together at 10:00 pm; Mom would handle the 1:30 am feed by herself; and Dad would handle the 5:00 am feed by himself. With this method, Mom and Dad could get a longer stretch of sleep each night.

Many families have the babies sleep in the same room initially and split the babies up later as needed, usually into boy or girl bedrooms for multi-gendered triplets.

Families with triplets realize the importance of reaching out to others and asking for help. Friends can help families organize meal programs; one family's church arranged a schedule to deliver meals to the house 3 times a week in the early months. Families find it

> ## *Triplet Tip!*
> Stash important supplies (diapers, burp cloths, and the like) in convenient places on each level of the home to minimize time spent running around retrieving necessary items.

helpful to give helpers and volunteers very specific instructions of what needs to be done (for example, how much to feed the baby, how often to pause for burp breaks, how long to hold upright after feeding) to minimize confusion.

> ## *Triplet Tip!*
> Volunteers are wonderful when your triplets are young. Don't be shy about making sure that your family's needs are met. There is enough chaos in your home as it is, and you should not hesitate to ask volunteers to please leave their own children at home when they come to help at your home. In addition, all volunteers should be healthy and virus-free to help your babies stay healthy.

Organizing the Triplet Way

Organizing bottles, nipples, and formula streamlines the feeding process. Many families buy supplies in bulk and store them in a designated location, to quickly assess what supplies are needed before embarking on another shopping trip.

Dry-erase boards are very useful for families with multiples. Many families use a dry-erase calendar to keep track of volunteers in the early months at home. Other families use large dry-erase bulletin boards to keep track of the triplets' feeds, wet and dirty diapers, moods, and medications. As your triplets grow older, the bulletin boards can transition to keep track of school calendars, assignments, and extracurricular schedules.

Triplet Tip!

One family with triplets and 3 older single-born children created a buddy system in case of emergencies such as a house fire—each older sibling was instructed to take her assigned baby and exit the house quickly if need be.

Another mother of older triplets keeps her smart phone on all the time. She programs in her children's appointments, school functions, and activities, and has the phone beep 24 hours ahead of time as reminders to keep her on schedule.

Color-coding helps families with multiples keep track of each child's items. Give each child a signature color starting in infancy to help identify personal items, and identify who each child is in pictures.

Toilet Training Triplets

Families with triplets often find toilet training 3 kids at once to be overwhelming for everyone involved. One family began potty training their triplets, 2 boys and a girl, at the same time, but as the mom describes it, "It was a circus!" They abandoned that idea and began training each child separately, starting with the child who showed the most signs of readiness, with much greater success. The extra one-on-one attention each child received with separate training led to better successes on the potty.

Interpersonal Relationships and Emotions

How can spouses support each other during triplets' early challenging months? Sleep deprivation affects everybody's mood and can have an effect on even the strongest of marriages. Many families find that a consistent, early bedtime for the children gives the parents some quality quiet time together. Other families squeeze in good spouse conversations whenever possible—even if at 3:00 am, if that is the only time that both parents are awake and together, with no disruptions.

When navigating the early years with triplets, a go-with-the-flow attitude really helps. Once one stage or schedule is mastered, things change and you need to adapt. Try to anticipate and be prepared for the triplets' next developmental stage.

Be realistic in what you can accomplish in one day. Lower your daily expectations if you must! The early months can be a haze of constant feeding and care—take things one day at a time. A calm parent is a more effective parent.

Try not to stress about giving each of your triplets identical experiences. Strive to be fair among your children instead. One mother of triplets noticed that one of her triplets hit his milestones a bit earlier than his siblings and was a bit more self-sufficient. It is now years later, yet she still feels twinges of guilt about him—she worries that he missed out on some of the mom-attention that his siblings received for being "needier." You cannot give your children identical experiences—you've just got to do your best to be fair, not equal.

Most families notice that as their triplets grow older, each child exhibits unique talents. Only one of a family's triplet sons excelled at baseball. They encouraged him and noticed that his self-esteem blossomed; his siblings participated in completely different activities. It is wise to not simply place all the kids in one single activity; encourage each child to find his special areas of interest.

❧ Benefits of Triplets

Triplets can be quite a team. They are socially savvy because they are always interacting with other children their own age. They always have each other and they tend to be quite outgoing in new social situations.

Being raised as a triplet provides plenty of built-in life lessons. Triplets have learned to share and be patient from infancy, by virtue of their family logistics! Triplet children have a less self-centered view of the world because they have siblings the same age.

☙ Maintaining Individuality

The importance of treating all your children as individuals, regardless of birthdays, cannot be overstated. One triplet family has a terrific method of ensuring weekly quality one-on-one time with each of the children. On Saturday mornings, Mom has a special outing with one child, Dad has an outing with another child, and the remaining children stay at home with a trusted babysitter. A rotating schedule is used to be fair to everyone and help the children know what to expect and when their special time is coming. Even in a large family, with a fair bit of planning and strategizing, families can spend quality one-on-one time with each of their children.

☙ The Adventure of a Lifetime!

Families with triplets agree that the early weeks and months are grueling, but are more than worth it to have their beautiful family. Organization and streamlining strategies will help families with triplets stay sane and happy. Enjoy each of your triplets' stages—soon the stage will be over and you will all be on to the next challenge!

Index